Olga Khomenko

The Faraway Sky of Kyiv
Ukrainians in the War

With a foreword by Hiroaki Kuromiya

UKRAINIAN VOICES

Collected by Andreas Umland

74 *Leonid Finberg*
   My Ukraine
   Rethinking the Past, Building the Present
   ISBN 978-3-8382-1974-5

75 *Joseph Zissels*
   Consider My Inmost Thoughts
   Essays, Lectures, and Interviews on Ukrainian Matters at the Turn of the Century
   ISBN 978-3-8382-1975-2

76 *Margarita Yehorchenko, Iryna Berlyand, Ihor Vinokurov (eds.)*
   Jewish Addresses in Ukraine
   A Guide-Book
   With a foreword by Leonid Finberg
   ISB 978-3-8382-1976-9

77 *Viktoriia Grivina*
   Kharkiv—A War City
   A Collection of Essays from 2022–23
   ISBN 978-3-8382-1988-2

78 *Hjørdis Clemmensen, Viktoriia Grivina, Vasylysa Shchogoleva*
   Kharkiv Is a Dream
   Public Art and Activism 2013–2023
   With a foreword by Bohdan Volynskyi
   ISBN 978-3-8382-2005-5

The book series "Ukrainian Voices" publishes English- and German-language monographs, edited volumes, document collections, and anthologies of articles authored and composed by Ukrainian politicians, intellectuals, activists, officials, researchers, and diplomats. The series' aim is to introduce Western and other audiences to Ukrainian explorations, deliberations and interpretations of historic and current, domestic, and international affairs. The purpose of these books is to make non-Ukrainian readers familiar with how some prominent Ukrainians approach, view and assess their country's development and position in the world. The series was founded, and the volumes are collected by Andreas Umland, Dr. phil. (FU Berlin), Ph. D. (Cambridge), Associate Professor of Politics at the Kyiv-Mohyla Academy and an Analyst in the Stockholm Centre for Eastern European Studies at the Swedish Institute of International Affairs.

Olga Khomenko

THE FARAWAY SKY OF KYIV
Ukrainians in the War

With a foreword by Hiroaki Kuromiya

Bibliografische Information der Deutschen Nationalbibliothek
Die Deutsche Nationalbibliothek verzeichnet diese Publikation in der Deutschen Nationalbibliografie; detaillierte bibliografische Daten sind im Internet über http://dnb.d-nb.de abrufbar.

Bibliographic information published by the Deutsche Nationalbibliothek
The Deutsche Nationalbibliothek lists this publication in the Deutsche Nationalbibliografie; detailed bibliographic data are available on the Internet at http://dnb.d-nb.de.

Book cover design by Yuliia Krylova
Cover photo by Valentyn Kuzan. Used with kind permission.
Translated from Japanese by Alina Kudina
Edited and updated by Olga Khomenko
Back cover photo by Akiko Tsunoda

This is the English language version of *Faraway Sky of Kyiv. Ukrainians in the War* previously published in Japanese. It has been revised, expanded and includes a new foreword by Hiroaki Kuromiya.

ISBN (Print): 978-3-8382-2006-2
ISBN (E-Book [PDF]): 978-3-8382-8006-6
© *ibidem*-Verlag, Hannover • Stuttgart 2025

Alle Rechte vorbehalten

Leuschnerstraße 40
30457 Hannover
info@ibidem.eu

Das Werk einschließlich aller seiner Teile ist urheberrechtlich geschützt. Jede Verwertung außerhalb der engen Grenzen des Urheberrechtsgesetzes ist ohne Zustimmung des Verlages unzulässig und strafbar. Dies gilt insbesondere für Vervielfältigungen, Übersetzungen, Mikroverfilmungen und elektronische Speicherformen sowie die Einspeicherung und Verarbeitung in elektronischen Systemen.

All rights reserved. No part of this publication may be reproduced, stored in or introduced into a retrieval system, or transmitted, in any form, or by any means (electronic, mechanical, photocopying, recording or otherwise) without the prior written permission of the publisher. Any person who commits any unauthorized act in relation to this publication may be liable to criminal prosecution and civil claims for damages.

Printed in the EU

Contents

Foreword by *Hiroaki Kuromiya* 7
Acknowledgments 11
Introduction 17

I. About that Day

1. A Premonition of War 27
2. Where is My Home? 32
3. Conversations with God 39
4. A War of Men, Women and Children 46
5. The War and Smartphones 52

II. A Country Called Ukraine

1. The Closest Country: Poland 61
2. The Two Seas of Ukraine 68
3. The Trauma of Ukrainian People 72
4. History of Migration 78
5. Flag of Blue Sky and Wheat Field 83

III. Daily Life During Wartime

1. War Expressed in Art 91
2. Laughing at War 97
3. On Everyday Life 100
4. Ukraine and Japan 105

IV. Losses and Gains

1. War and Friendship 115
2. The Heroes of Our Time 119
3. Taras Shevchenko, National Poet 128
4. War and Business 136
5. Friends on the Other Side 146

Conclusion: Thoughts of Ukrainians on Homeland and Borders 157

Foreword

Ukraine is at once well-known and little-known in the anglophone world. Ukrainian Cossacks are sometimes dubbed "Ukrainian Cowboys," making them instantly recognizable to the American public, in particular through the 1962 American film "Taras Bulba" starring Tony Curtis and Yul Brynner. Few Westerners know the difference between Ukrainian and Russian Cossacks and the film itself confuses the two, as well as, for that matter, Ukraine and Russia in general. This is a common problem of perception for Ukraine. Ukraine's geographical and historical presence may be apparent in the consciousness of the world, but it has always been largely—at times totally—eclipsed by its gigantic eastern neighbor: Russia. In popular and even political and academic discourse Ukraine's distinct identity has been dissolved in the imperialist identity of Russia; somewhat similar to the way in which popular discourse often substitutes "England" for Great Britain (which of course includes Scotland, Wales, and Northern Ireland). It is of note that the film "Taras Bulba" is loosely based on an eponymous 19th century Russian-language novel by Mykola Hohol, a Ukrainian writer whom most readers know better by his Russian name Nikolai Gogol—thus inaccurately identifying him as Russian.

It is not that Ukraine has left its legitimate rights unclaimed. At least since the 19th century, it has done so loudly and with vigour against all usurpers, most importantly Russia. The Ukrainian diaspora communities have been active and vocal, particularly in North America. In the aftermath of World War One, the world, led by the US President Woodrow Wilson, acknowledged the principle of the "self-determination" of nations, allowing for the independence of many European countries (Poland, Czechoslovakia, Yugoslavia, Finland, the Baltic States, and others). Yet Ukraine, like Belarus, Central Asia, and other Russian imperialist possessions, was not recognized to be a nation worthy of "self-determination." The question did not concern the Russian Empire alone, however.

Neither Ireland nor India was recognized at the time in view of the interests of the British Empire. Imperialist interests still predominated in the world at the time.

It took a second World War to put an end to the age of empire. Following the defeat of the late-comer empire—Germany, Italy, and Japan—the world witnessed the independence of their former colonies, as well as those of the more established empires of Britain, France, the Netherlands, Belgium, and others. The Russian Empire (re-branded as the Soviet Union in 1922) was the exception. It was only in 1991 that the Russian Empire collapsed and Ukraine and other Russian colonial possessions (including the Baltic States, Georgia, Armenia, and Kazakhstan) became independent. At long last Ukraine acquired the opportunity to extract itself from Russian rule.

Yet Ukraine, like many other countries, suffered from the politics of the great powers. By no means is Ukraine small, certainly larger in both population and geographical area than its sizable neighbor in the west—Poland. Nevertheless, Ukraine has often been sacrificed to the interests of the great powers. In the aftermath of the collapse of the Soviet Union, Ukraine, along with Belarus and Kazakhstan, agreed to renounce the Soviet nuclear weapons they had possessed in exchange for a guarantee of security and territorial integrity (the so-called Budapest Agreement of 1994 signed by Washington, London, and Moscow). When Russia blatantly violated the agreement and invaded Ukraine under false cover, annexing Crimea and occupying large segments of the Donbas in eastern Ukraine, the United States and Britain failed to honor the agreement. Russia's implicit nuclear blackmail had worked, and Ukraine's security and territorial integrity were sacrificed. The West's tepid reaction to Moscow's imperialist aggression created the necessary conditions for Russia's full-scale invasion of Ukraine in February 2022.

The world has seen Ukraine fight gallantly and tenaciously against the Russian invaders. The war has also opened the world's eyes to Ukraine. Yet there is still much to learn about this country.

Olga Khomenko's sensitive and moving essays collected in this book sketch one Ukrainian's journey through the pain, despair, hope, and faith every Ukrainian must have experienced in one way or another in the war Russia unleashed against Ukraine.

From these deeply personal and subtle accounts of the war, several general messages can be heard. Ukraine is not Russia, their linguistic, cultural, and historical ties notwithstanding. In its fight for autonomy, Ukraine does not ask for pity. It asks for whatever support the world can offer — military, political, economic, and emotional. With, or even without, it, Ukraine will determine its own future, rejecting Russia's interference. Ukraine's legendary spirit of courage, fortitude, and independence shines through these pages.

An academic Japanologist trained in Japan, the author originally wrote these essays in Japanese for the Japanese reader, and this English version is translated from the original Japanese. Japan's engagement with Ukraine may not have been as close as that of Europe or America. Yet in certain respects Japan has been keenly aware of Ukraine's significance. Already, before 1905, Japan had Ukraine in mind (as well as Poland, Finland, and other captive nations in the Russian Empire) as a potential force to weaken the empire from within. Nevertheless, the popular understanding of Ukraine in Japan, like that in the West, tends to be shallow and superficial and heavily prejudiced by Russocentric views common even in academic circles. The original Japanese version published in the summer of 2023 has been lauded in Japan as a means to better understand Ukraine, its history, culture, people, and above all, its existential fight against an invading Russia. The English edition is likely to have a similar impact on the anglophone world.

Dr Hiroaki Kuromiya
Emeritus Professor of History at
Indiana University in Bloomington

Acknowledgments

I never planned to write a memoir about wartime; I always felt too young for such an endeavor. But war does not wait for us to be ready. As a professionally trained historian and Asianist with extensive education in Japan, I wrote these essays to process my feelings and trauma from the war and ensure that these experiences are not lost to memory. Japanese holds a special place in my heart because I was educated in Japan, so I initially wrote this book in that language. I also wanted to share my story with my former classmates and teachers in Japan, who had been concerned about how I was doing. As a scholar and intellectual, I felt a professional responsibility to share this firsthand account with Japan. Also, for more than twenty years I worked as an independent freelance producer and coordinator for major Japanese TV channels, creating documentaries, news reports and TV programs. So, I know very well the processes in newsrooms. That was also one of the reasons why I decided to give my people a voice to speak for themselves.

The book was first published in the summer of 2023, and to my surprise, it was met with overwhelmingly positive feedback. Amazon Japan at one point even ranked it among the top 10 books on foreign countries. With the English translation complete, I am eager to share these reflections with a broader audience.

I would also like to thank everyone who supported me during my journey. First, I would like to thank CARA (Council for Researchers at Risk), the British Academy, and the University of Oxford for allowing me to continue my studies peacefully. I would like to express my sincere gratitude to Professor Sho Konishi, Nissan Institute of Japanese Studies and Professor Paul Chaisty, and St. Antony's College, who kindly accepted me as a fellow and provided their advice, support and friendship. I will never forget it. I would also like to thank Professor Roger Goodman, Professor Hugh Whittaker, Professor Takehiko Kariya, and Ms. Jane Baker for their kindness, guidance and support.

I am also deeply thankful to Junko Imanishi, who first asked me why I did not write about my experience and kindly published my writings in the monthly magazine of Atsumi International Foundation. I am also grateful to the Japanese publishing house Chuo Koron Shinsha, which published it first as a book in Japanese.

I can't express enough gratitude to Will Medd, a professional certified coach, who worked with us on CVs, self-advocacy and presentation at one of the CARA seminars and encouraged me to translate my book into English. I also want to thank my friend Mattias Williams for his friendship in Kyiv during his years as head of Reuters' Ukrainian office, for being the first reader of the English version, and for encouraging me to publish it.

I am enormously thankful to Professor Serhii Plokhy, my mentor at Harvard during my Fulbright scholarship, whose academic and personal advice has always greatly supported and influenced me. I am also very thankful to Professor Hiroaki Kuromiya, who wrote a very kind and thoughtful foreword for this book and has supported my studies since my fellowship in the USA.

Special thanks to my former student, William Mitchell Reid, for reading this book and giving his kind feedback. Also, I am deeply grateful to my friends Ashley Woods, his wife Wendy Ko and children Maya and Tyler for opening their home and hearts in London for my mother and I.

I would like to express my sincere gratitude to Oleksandr Savruk and Kyiv Mohyla Business School and to Serhii Kvit and National University of Kyiv Mohyla Academy for their support.

I am also very thankful to Professor Andreas Umland, the editor of the book series "Ukrainian Voices," and the entire Ibidem team for publishing this book.

My special gratitude to Sally Spode for her invaluable assistance in editing this book. Your dedication and meticulous attention to detail have made this work so much better. Thank you!

I would like to extend my gratitude to Valentyn Kuzan for the stunning cover photo of this book. The image captures his son, born just months before the war, gazing up at the Kyiv sky—a poignant representation of countless children experiencing their childhood amidst the challenges of wartime Ukraine.

A heartfelt thank you to Yuliia Krylova, my talented former student and the creative mind behind this book's stunning cover design. I also extend my deepest gratitude to Akiko Tsunoda, a gifted photographer and dear friend, for capturing such a beautiful portrait of me. Your contributions have truly elevated this project—without you, it would not be the same.

I would also like to express my heartfelt gratitude to all my friends and colleagues around the globe who have been there for me and supported me through the past two and a half years: Zbig Wojnowski, Marcel Garbos, Koji Tsunoda, Tetyana Papernyuk, Olga Nagy and her family, Annamaria Szentes and Peter Borbas, Hannes and Helga Hassler, as well as Hannes' parents, Tatsuo Kamino, Andrea Matusch and her husband Heinz, Emanuel, Erich and Elisabeth Zillner, professor Wolfram Manzenreiter and professor Inna Hein from Vienna University, Marta and Kevin Grieve, Mira Sonntag, Mao Wada and her husband Richard, Olena Vovk and Filip Visic, Oksana, Dasha and Aleksei Kondratyev, Anelia Neganova and her husband Vasyl, Kateryna and Serhiy Grunt, Markiyan Kychma, Valya Khomenko, Vitaliy Khomenko, Ivan Khomenko, Sophia Podkolzina, Sasha Petrauskaite, Max Sviezhentsev, Oleksandr Nechytailo, Serhiy Lokot, Oksana and Oleg Kirichek, Marat Gaifullin, Nataliya Kibita, Natalia Khanenko-Friesen, Serge Cipko, Ogata Kenichi and his wife Yumi, Sonoko Hirose, Michiko Kanda, Yoshiaki and Yumi Nohara, Saki Ouchi, Masanobu Miyoshi, Yuko Demura, Junichi Sato, Ryosuke Kondo, Norihiro Naganawa, Hirayama Noboru, Makoto Okawa, Masamichi Ogawara, Taku Uchiyama, Wakana Kono, Noriko Unno, Yuichiro Shimizu, Yasuyuki Ishiga, Motokazu Matsutani, Shinya Shimada, professor Hidehiko Sekizawa, professor Kazuo Nakai and his wife—professor Ayako Nakai, professor Yoko Iwama, professor Kyoko Numano, professor Iryna Matyash, Etsuko Fujii, Yumiko Toda, Bota Usen, Taro Tsurumi, Tatiana Linkhoeva, Svitlana Pyrkalo, Marina Pesenti, Serge Kovela, Sergiy Nizhinskyi, Olha Pryymak, Andriy Naumov, Alice Freeman, Alice Baldock, Chinami Oka, Martina Baradel, Mioko Nari, Anna Sharko, Fabio

Gygi, Shilla Lee, Jessica Zychowicz, Vasyl Lopukh, Igor Serdiuk, Kateryna Kovalchuk, Yaryna Pikh and Oleksandr Avramchuk, Mariia Rybalchenko, Dana Gritane, Alexey Volokhov, Martin Dambergs, Andrejs and Daina Ekis, Vasiliy Sych, Iryna Zaloha, Marta Shevchenko, Inna Shvorak, Marianna Motrunych, Lida Sirenko and Lesyk Yakymchuk and many others. Your encouragement, companionship, and unwavering support have been invaluable, and I am deeply grateful to each of you. Thank you for all your help, encouraging words, talks, telephone calls, dinners and places to sleep which you provided for me.

I hope that by reading this book, international readers will understand the feelings that were in the hearts of Ukrainians after February 24th, 2022, and the social and economic changes that took place. A friend of mine, a psychiatrist, jokingly told me that every patient who comes to them these days wishes they could "return to the reality of February 23rd, the day before the war", but that is impossible. We must somehow get used to this new reality.

I certainly do not want to retrace the painful path we have been on since February 24th, but I have decided to do it one more time with the readers of this book, to let the readers to know what changes have taken place in the hearts of the Ukrainian people. Thank you for reading this book and thank you for supporting Ukraine and Ukrainians.

Writing this book was an emotionally challenging journey for me. However, it was essential to give a global voice to my people. Initially, I considered translating the work myself but found it too overwhelming. I recalled reading an essay by Jhumpa Lahiri call "In Other Words"[1] where she explained how her way of expression changes between languages, so she never translated her own work: I resonate with that sentiment. Given how deeply personal and painful this book is, I wanted to avoid retraumatizing myself by revisiting those memories during translation. I am incredibly thankful to Alina Kudina for handling the translation and allowing me to focus solely on editing. Even then, the process was still emotionally complex. I hope you enjoy reading.

---

1   Jhumpa Lahiri. In other words. Translated by Ann Goldstein.-Bloomsbury Publishing, 2017.

To my mother, my students and all brave Ukrainian women and men.

Introduction

I was about ten years old. I was in art school, and I still remember my art history teacher showing me Japanese *sumi-e* (ink painting) and *hanga* (wood block prints), which made a strong impression on me. I thought it was a mysterious world; different from European art. I thought that someday I would like to visit the country that created that world. However, I lived in the Soviet Union behind the Iron Curtain, in Ukraine, so I knew that a trip to Japan was an unrealistic dream.

My father worked for a publishing house and my mother was a Ukrainian language teacher, so I grew up surrounded by books. When I looked for Japanese literature that had been translated, I first came across Japanese folktales in Ukrainian. Again, it was a strange world, and I was incredibly surprised. In Ukrainian folktales, the good guys and the bad guys are clearly defined, and the bad guys always lose in the end. In Japanese stories, this is not always the case. I also found it surprising that even though the villains existed, not all of their actions were evil. But at that time, having never seen a foreigner, let alone a Japanese person, distant Japan was a complete dream world for me. Even if I wanted to learn about Japan, there were barriers that I could not overcome.

In the former Soviet Union, Japanese language study was exclusively reserved for men, with classes limited to an extremely small number of children of leaders related to the Communist Party. Women were not often accepted for jobs where they could make use of their Japanese, such as in the military or security services. Those women who were allowed were an exceptional group. Since the country was separated by the Iron Curtain, the Communists were convinced that they were surrounded by enemies. Thus, the only purpose of having them learn foreign languages was to gain an advantage for the country: the Soviet Union. Namely, it was for information gathering, such as espionage; and to spread Soviet culture, primarily the Russian language, abroad.

Even for those interested in foreign cultures, learning Japanese, a unique foreign language, was a dream that was out of reach. This was even more inconceivable for a child like me, who spoke Ukrainian daily and came from a so-called "intelligentsia family" whose parents supported Ukrainian culture. I was neither affiliated with the Communist Party, nor was I a worshipper of mainstream Russian culture. Since elementary school, I had also attended Ukrainian language school — only about 5 percent of the schools taught in Ukrainian compared to the number of schools teaching in Russian — and was bilingual, speaking Ukrainian as my home language and Russian outside, of course.

However, my love of writing and my desire to become a journalist or writer led me to enroll in the Faculty of Philology at Kyiv National University in the hope of getting a broader basic education. At that time, the Department of Ukrainian Philology was not exceedingly popular. There were only 40 students in their two courses. Back then, Kyiv University was one of the few places where one could gain expertise to go abroad, only the children of important people were allowed to enter, and we had Russian as a foreign language classes. On the other hand, people studying in Ukrainian came from an almost identical family background. My friends' parents were writers, playwrights, and schoolteachers: people who were closer to the unofficial culture than to the public stage in Soviet Union. The Ukrainian language was considered a rural language by Soviet policy. However, the year I entered the university (1989), a reversal was made, and the Law on National Language was established, which legally recognized the role of Ukrainian (it became the national language). By the time I finished my sophomore year (August 24th, 1991), Ukraine finally became an independent country.

The popularity of and need for the Ukrainian language increased after independence, and from the following year, about 100 students were enrolled every year in the Department of Ukrainian Philology. Then the Department of Oriental Languages was established in the Faculty of Letters, where students could freely study not only Ukrainian as a major, but also various Asian languages — such as Chinese, Japanese, Arabic, Hebrew, and

Korean. When I learnt this, I remembered the Japanese artworks my teacher had shown me when I was a child and thought without hesitation: 'I will learn Japanese'. However, Japanese is a complex language for Ukrainians who are not part of the so-called "hieroglyphic (or *kanji* in Japanese) world" to which Japan and China belong. When I started studying there were about 60 classmates, but when I graduated there were only two of us left.

In the beginning, my friends and relatives laughed at me a lot, saying "These (kanji characters) are like pictures, so it is difficult to study them. You should stop wasting your time. If you choose English or German, you will be able to learn faster." But I did not heed such advice and frantically wrote kanji characters on A4 paper and stuck them all over the house. My parents smiled with curiosity. In 1992 — the year I started drafting this book (2022) marks the 30th anniversary — diplomatic relations were established between Ukraine and Japan, and a Japanese embassy was opened in Kyiv, opening the way for me to further my studies in Japan.

I pursued the path of journalism and started working part-time at a newspaper in my second year of university. In addition to that, in my fourth year (back then one had to study for five years at Ukrainian universities), I worked for about a year as an observer in the political department of UNIAN, the newly founded and largest news agency in Ukraine. I had a momentary hesitation about quitting my Japanese studies and pursuing journalism in Ukraine, but I decided to give priority to my studies abroad in Japan. I am glad I did.

The first experience of my studies abroad was in Ryukoku University in Kyoto, a Buddhist university, where I made many discoveries. For example, one of my tennis club mates was a son of a Buddhist monk, which was unbelievable in Ukraine. Typically, the daily routines of children of Orthodox clergymen are well-structured, and playing tennis is not usually part of their activities.

On Friday afternoons I had Japanese class, and my teacher was a kind old man who gave us still warm *taiyaki*[2], when we had done our homework well. Even now I remember his kindness when I eat *taiyaki*. As a newly independent nation, Ukraine faced severe economic challenges, including high inflation and rapidly shrinking savings. Our teacher likely understood this struggle and wanted to make our Fridays a little brighter.

After studying Japanese for about five hours every day, I would climb to the top of Fushimi Inari Shrine to refresh myself. It was before the *senbon-torii*[3] gate became famous, so there were no tourists at all, and the statue of a fox in the middle of the path was a bit scary. I selfishly almost thought of it as my own private garden. Now I am surprised every time by the number of tourists at Fushimi Inari Shrine.

After my year at Ryukoku University, I returned to Ukraine, graduated from Kyiv State University and decided to continue my studies in Japan a little longer, taking a one-year programme at Ritsumeikan University's College of International Relations. At this time, I lived in an International House near Hanazono Station, which was a broadly cosmopolitan environment. Having grown up behind the Iron Curtain, I now made friends from Australia, the USA, France, Germany and Argentina for the first time, and lived with them for a year. Breaking new ground, my American friends and I talked about the Cold War era and I learnt that as children they used to watch television and were scared that the Soviet Union would drop bombs on them; meanwhile I was scared of the opposite, that the US would be dropping bombs on us. We laughed at each other. My friends are now lawyers, teachers, employees of international organisations and musicians,

---

2   *Taiyaki* is a popular Japanese street food, a cake that is shaped like a fish, specifically a sea bream (called "*tai*" in Japanese, which symbolizes good luck). It's a type of filled cake made from a pancake-like batter, cooked in fish-shaped molds. Traditionally, *taiyaki* is filled with *anko*, a sweet red bean paste made from adzuki beans.

3   Means "thousand gates" in English. *Senbon-torii* refers to a specific and iconic feature found in certain Shinto shrines in Japan, particularly at the famous Fushimi Inari Taisha in Kyoto.

and we still keep in touch. I discovered a whole new universe in Kyoto that year: a fearless, borderless world.

After the Ritsumeikan programme, I got a job at the Ministry of Foreign Affairs of Ukraine and worked as a third secretary and cultural attaché at the Ukrainian Embassy in Japan. Later, I continued my studies at the graduate school of Kyiv National University and at the University of Tokyo, where I undertook research at the Graduate School of Arts and Sciences and began to study history, political thought and philosophy in greater detail. I have fond memories of discussing not only my research topics but also many other subjects with my colleagues in seminars and lecture courses, as well as well as going shopping for second-hand books in the Kanda area of Tokyo.

I was still in the master's program not even ten years after Ukraine's independence, so I was interested in the history of ideas, nation-building, education and scholarship in Japan's Meiji period (1868 -1912). I thought that Japan's experience would be useful for Ukraine in its formation as a nation. With this in mind, I researched Fukuzawa Yukichi's writings, especially his theory of learning and the formation of morals, which influenced the development of the educational system in modern Japan. During my doctoral studies, I shifted my research focus towards the postwar history of Japan, media history, consumption, and marketing. Inspired by Ukraine's ongoing transition to a capitalist economic system, I explored how media and advertising influenced the behavior of postwar Japanese consumers. Both of these experiences helped me in my academic and professional lives as a scholar, media producer and writer.

Ukraine's independence paved the way for my new life. My relations with Japan are entirely thanks to Ukraine's independence. Without it, I would not have had the opportunity to learn Japanese and to study abroad in Japan. Nor would I have introduced Ukrainian culture to Japan.

Almost 30 years have passed since I started studying Japanese, and I cherish my relationship with Japan. Not only I have been able to introduce Japanese history and culture in Ukraine, but I have also introduced Ukrainian history, literature and culture in Japan. In this context, in 2005 together with Etsuko Fujii I co-translated an *"Anthology of Modern Ukrainian Literature"*, in 2014 I published my collection of essays "From Ukraine with Love", and almost three weeks before the Russian invasion I published a collection of essays entitled "Ukrainians Beyond Borders". The title of this book only seemed fateful, as I myself became a *"Ukrainian Beyond Borders"*. The subject of the book is people born in Ukraine who have moved around the world by being displaced, such as immigrants, refugees or asylum seekers, and have developed their talents in spite of their difficult historical circumstances.

When Russia launched its invasion of Ukraine on 24th February 2022, I was visiting friends in Vienna. I never thought in my nightmares that the number of Ukrainian refugees crossing the border after that day would exceed 6 million people. I never thought that my research on Ukrainian emigrants and their community outside the country would come to life and become part of my life. It was a frightening development.

After the Russian offensive started, the Japanese media told many stories about Ukraine. However, I thought that there were still stories that could not be told there, so I decided to publish this collection of essays. How do Ukrainians perceive this reality and their own historical past, and how are they trying to move on? What are they thinking about as they live their daily lives?

Since the onset of the Russian invasion, I received numerous interview requests from Japanese media. However, I began declining all of them. Most outlets asked the same questions: What do you think of the current situation? How do you feel? I came to see that dealing with the realities of the war, helping family and friends to evacuate, and being expected to reflect on how I feel about it would only make things worse. I was not in a position to either reflect on or answer the questions. I needed some time to digest it all.

- We are told that every year around May, Kyiv becomes a city of blooming chestnuts and filled with romantic scents. How do you feel about not being able to spend this time of year in Kyiv due to the war?

- In your previous book, you wrote that Ukrainians have a special attachment to the land because Ukraine was originally a country of farmers. I also found out that your great-grandfather had his land confiscated by the Soviet Union after the Russian Revolution. Considering that, is it a particularly painful experience for Ukrainians to be forced to leave their land these days?

Just reading these things made me feel sick, as the view of Kyiv filled with chestnut flowers and the landscapes of my great-grandfather's place flashed before my eyes. This man said he was a reporter for a prestigious Japanese magazine, but all I could think was that anyone who would ask such questions had no heart. I was not the only one who got asked such questions. When I asked acquaintances who had been interviewed by the Japanese media, they said the interviewers were similarly callous.

There was one story that was utterly beyond my understanding. An elderly mother who lost her son in Bucha was interviewed on the street by the Japanese media, and after repeating several times "How did you feel at that time?" the woman left in tears in the middle of the interview. It is not hard to understand. The media wants sensational stories. I have extensive experience in international and Japanese media, so I know what it is like to work there, but this is the first time I have been the subject of an interview, and I realized many things.

In all honesty, I did not want to talk to others about this.

I decided to decline all interviews and write in my own voice to give a voice to my people. I thought it would cause less psychological damage. I thought that writing it myself would, in a sense, help me process my feelings and get over the trauma. When I actually saw my friend being tossed aside after some TV interview, I thought again that I had made the right decision. The Japanese media's attention span is short and news is consumed rapidly.

Ukraine has been a listener, not a narrator, for hundreds of years, but I think the time has come for that situation to change. All who spoke about Ukrainian history and language were foreigners, and until the 19th century, all who mapped Ukraine were also foreigners. But it is time to graduate from being a listener and become the storyteller.

Being alive means
To be alive now
To be able to cry
To be able to laugh
To be able to be angry
To be free
Shuntaro Tanikawa, Ikiru, 1971

I. About that Day

1. A Premonition of War

I'm on a train running through the Austrian countryside. The scenery outside the window is full of spring flowers, and their beauty makes my heart flutter. Today is the first time I am going to see my family who were able to evacuate to Austria.

I had come to Vienna on a trip two weeks before the war started. My mother and sister's family, who lived in the capital Kyiv, decided to leave the city on February 25th, after the bombing began and after spending the night in a cold shelter in the school's basement (in Ukraine, all schools from elementary to high school are in the same building).

Leaving town was by no means safe; they were even unsure which road to take. After consulting with a friend in western Ukraine, they opted for the general road between villages instead of the main highway connecting Kyiv to the western city of Lviv. The trip by highway usually took six to seven hours, but they arrived in Lviv after 28 hours due to traffic congestion. Even so, they were able to refuel on the way and were lucky to get out of Kyiv without being attacked by an airstrike.

My student Polina's family, who also lives in Kyiv, was not that lucky. On the same February the 25th, they drove west in the direction of Zhytomyr and were soon stuck in a traffic jam. Furthermore, they returned to Kyiv once they heard air strikes on the Hostomel airport northwest of Kyiv. Giving up on trying to escape by car, the next day they went to the Kyiv railway station to take the train, but it was so crowded that they could not get on it. Polina began to stammer under stress and some of her hair turned grey. Fortunately, two weeks later she was able to go to her father's place in Poland.

In fact, it took my family only 40 minutes to leave once they had decided to do so. They did not have any time to prepare. The people of Kyiv who had anticipated the war were starting to prepare evacuation bags in January. Amongst other things, these bags contained: passports, driving licenses, underwear, socks, food bars, drinking water, batteries, portable radios and phone chargers. This evacuation bag is the same as an emergency kit for earthquakes in Japan. But instead of an earthquake, there was war. I never thought I would experience such a thing in my life.

While preparing my evacuation bag, I read an action manual for the first time entitled "In Case of Air Strikes," distributed by Ukrainian defense ministry in 2014 at the beginning of the war in eastern Ukraine. I learned that the bathroom is the safest place in the house because it has load-bearing walls, no windows, and is structurally most likely to save lives even if bombed. In reality, this was not always the case.

My mother did not make an evacuation bag until the very last minute. She disregarded talk of war. Therefore, when the time came for her to leave the house she was quite flustered. This was because she not only needed her own belongings, but also food and medicine for her dog. She managed to pack her things; but left wearing her oldest shoes. When I met my mother again later, she spoke to me sadly, "You bought me so many shoes, why did I wear the oldest ones?"

I guess my mother did not make an evacuation bag, not because she was careless, but rather because she did not want to believe that a war would break out. She was over 80 years old and had already experienced war as a child. Since the end of January, my mother's friend who was living in Europe had been asking her to visit them (this was a euphemistic invitation to evacuate), but she had strongly refused. She did not believe a war would come into our homes.

An Overactive Imagination?

It was not only the elderly who believed that war would not happen, but the young as well, and many of them were optimistic about the situation.

A friend of mine, on returning home for Orthodox Christmas on January 7th said, "It's strange that the American and European media are making such a fuss about the imminent war, but the people of Kyiv are in a festive mood and have forgotten the reality of the situation". My family in Kyiv, also laughing at me, said, "You have an overactive imagination. There will never be a war." Looking back on it, it was not funny.

In Kyiv in the second half of January, tensions were rising in places we could not see. Foreign embassies were beginning to withdraw, and Japanese trading company employees were sending their families back home. After that, foreigners gradually began to move to neighboring European countries. I was in Kyiv at the time and felt abandoned as all my friends left.

On January 25th, the Japanese government raised Ukraine to travel danger level 4. This meant "Please evacuate. Do not travel there."

At 5:00 a.m. on the morning of the next day, the 26th I received an urgent e-mail from a Japanese company with which I had a meeting scheduled for that day. Without a single word of greeting, it simply said, "All operations are suspended." From that day on, everyone disappeared.

When I told this to a Japanese friend, he said, "This is normal. It was the same during the wars in Iraq and Afghanistan. They want to get everyone back home before things get really bad. It would cost a lot of money to fly a government-chartered plane later." I was surprised when they mentioned it so calmly. I never thought that Ukraine would be the same as Iraq or Afghanistan, but I was naïve in my thinking.

At the end of January, there were many reports in the foreign media that the people of Kyiv were courageous and would not leave. Was it courage, or was it just that we did not let our anxiety show on our faces, or that we were unable to articulate our fears? Looking back, I think that many people around me were nervous and anxious. I was thinking about what I would do in case things went wrong, but I did not say it aloud.

Ukrainians tend to hold back until the last minute. It is like the Japanese, who avoid losing face in public and force themselves to be strong until the last minute. No matter how nervous we are, we try not to reveal our true feelings in public. Fake it until you make it, as the saying goes.

I once had an acquaintance who wrote about this trait of Ukrainians in social media. She wrote the following in an entertaining way: "Folks, I'm the type of person who cannot catch the vibe and does not realize things until the last minute. I am afraid I will miss some vital information in this situation, so if it comes down to it, someone please let me know. Please give me a nudge. Please give me a pat on the head, too." That woman is from northern city Chernihiv, located near the border with Belarus, and currently resides in Germany: someone must have given her that "nudge".

The Barriers to Evacuation to a Foreign Country

I am involved in many international research projects, so I am always ready to go on a business trip abroad. Passport, insurance card, credit cards, cash, laptop and mobile phone and their chargers — all ready to go. As long as I have the necessary contacts, I can buy everything else. However, there are few Ukrainians like me, and it is not easy for people who are not used to travelling to leave their homes. Furthermore, they become refugees in the places where they stay. There are many barriers to leaving the country and the biggest obstacle must be money. Ukrainians have not trusted banks since the collapse of the Soviet Union, so there are many domestic stashes of cash, therefore, there are many burglars and thieves.

Obviously, not everyone has a lot of savings. This is especially true for young people. Since the outbreak of COVID-19, unemployment has risen, and emergency moneylending has increased. People could borrow an amount of about 500–1000-euro equivalent, using their own houses or cars as collateral. However, this is not the case for the elderly. They have experienced many unconventional times, so they always have money for contingencies and funeral expenses. But still, despite the value of Ukrainian hryvnia falling by a fifth in 2014, when Russia invaded Crimea, few elderly people converted it into foreign currency.

What about the language barrier? Many Ukrainians who have sought refuge in foreign countries are not able to speak foreign languages. If they feel they are in grave danger, they will move just to survive.

In mid-March, I met such people at Vienna's main railway station. They lived in the north-eastern city of Sumy near the Russian border, but when a missile fell 100 meters from their house on February 24th, they packed hastily and took the train with their two children. Their destination was Spain. They said their daughter's relatives were living there. These were people for whom fear was the driving force for their migration.

Leaving their hard-earned home is another major barrier. The next section will cover Ukrainians' attachment to home. In short, home is the only asset they have. There is also the assumption that "No one would welcome us in a foreign country, we would only get problems if we went there." In addition, there are some people who have traumas and obstacles that they cannot share.

The idea of remaining at home, even after an air strike, is not difficult to understand. Older people want to remain in their own homes, surrounded by the things that shaped their lives. Elderly people like these exist in every country.

Two months have already passed since I left my home in Kyiv. When I went to Europe in mid-February, I obviously brought only the bare essentials. The season changed and I bought new spring and summer clothes. Yet what I have discovered is that the house does not really matter. As long as I am fine, I can build as many new homes as I want. But if I lose my life, this will be the end.

(8 May 2022)

2. Where is My Home?

What is Home for You?

When people ask me: "Where do you live?", I hesitate. I left my home and became a refugee because of the war. Yet, even in ordinary times if were to ask me: "What does home mean to you? Where do you live?" I might not be able to answer immediately.

There are many different answers to the question "What does home mean to you?" For some, it is their family home, where they go for Christmas and Easter vacations, eat their mother's cooking and recall childhood memories. It may be a place where your heart lies. For others, it is a home that they bought with their long and hard-earned efforts. Some people may call their home any place since they are carrying it in their travel bag, and some reply with a chuckle "On the plane."

I asked my friends, and they answered that it is where their partners, their families, their children are, and where their beloved dog is. There was also: "It is a place where we all get together and have a good time." One older person said: "My place is the kitchen where I can slowly cook and the bathroom where I can relax and unwind." Indeed, a house can be a place, certain things or people, or even a feeling. After the outbreak of COVID-19 in 2020 everyone began to reconsider the physical meaning of their homes. Many people have carefully reassessed their living environment since they began working from home. Even those who had previously used their homes exclusively as "places to sleep," also had to reconsider the meaning of home. I have also been reconsidering it over the past two years, to the point where I no longer want to think about it.

A friend of mine who works for a law company that deals with foreign investments was mostly away from Kyiv because of her frequent business trips before the outbreak of COVID-19. She was a person who carries her "home" in a suitcase for business trips. However, she bought a house right before the beginning of the COVID-19 pandemic. When I asked her why she bought it, she replied: "I want my own space where I can freely scatter my socks all over the place and no one will complain about it." I thought that that answer was somehow understandable.

Thoughts of Ukrainians on home

Ukrainians have a special feeling for their homes. This is evident both in the cities and in the countryside. Even in decades-old residential buildings, the entrances and the hallways may be old, but once you enter the apartment, you will find that it is beautifully maintained. People like to spend time at home, invite guests, and take good care of their "own homes".

Before the Russian Revolution, historians and ethnographers traveled through Ukraine and mentioned that Ukrainian and Russian villages are quite different from each other. In Ukraine, houses have gardens with flowers around them, and walls are repainted every year. The inside of the house is also beautiful; if Ukrainians earn any money, they invest it in their houses. The further west you go, the owners become wealthier and the houses become more beautiful.

During the Soviet era, when private property was prohibited under socialism, the house was the only asset people were allowed to have. Buying a car was a challenge, and they were not that widespread. The house had great moral significance; it was the only place to escape from societal pressure. No matter how much the government tried they could not control what people talked about in the kitchen or in their bedrooms. The house was the last remaining place where one could freely enjoy life. This was especially true of the kitchen, which was not only a place to have breakfast and supper, but where everyone gathered to talk. In Ukraine there is a strong attachment to home, with the kitchen as the centerpiece, to the extent that it is said that one can tell what kind of person lives in a house by looking at their kitchen.[4]

---

4   A friend of mine in the UK told me he was shocked when he saw on TV that a kitchen with the exact same layout as his was destroyed in one of the buildings in Irpin. He took it very personally and, in that moment, the war felt

After the Russian invasion on February 24th, 2022, I found myself once again thinking about my home. I had to suddenly leave the house where I had spent the two years after the COVID-19 outbreak reaching the point of being fed up with it. In an instant, I was deprived of the home that I had made by myself, including all the interiors, one by one, after much thought and effort. Even though my home still exists physically, I cannot express the emotional pain of not being able to return there. I never thought I would be forced to make such a hard choice: to stay at home, be hit by a missile and die, or to leave home and stay alive.

Not only in the current situation, but in the past as well Ukrainians have faced dangerous situations that required them to leave their homes. One example was the Chornobyl nuclear disaster in April 1986. Almost all the women and children in Kyiv were displaced from their homes that summer. I managed to return to my home in Kyiv at the end of August, and it felt incredible to be able to live a normal life again.

In the fall of 2013, when the then President Yanukovych abandoned the path to European Union membership, many young people thought about leaving home. One friend announced to his parents that "when the time comes, I will leave the country." His mother sat down by the carpet on the wall, which used to be a symbol of wealth, and asked: "But what are you going to do with this house?" My friend then replied: "However nice the house is with its carpets; freedom is more important. I don't want this apartment full of stale carpets in a *khrushchevka*[5] built in the 1960s anymore, I would rather be poor but free."

Another friend put money she had saved to buy a large sofa into a contingency fund in case she had to flee the country. Fortunately, after the Revolution of Dignity in February 2014[6]

---

incredibly close to him, as if his own house had been destroyed. This is a small detail how you feel a connection to what happening around the globe.

5   Small size apartments build during Nikita Khrushchev time in order to fulfil the growing needs for housing.

6   A massive anti-government protest after president Viktor Yanukovych refused to sign an Association Agreement with the EU, which ended with the ousting of Yanukovych who then fled to Russia.

Yanukovych defected and the regime changed, so her savings were intact.

A few years later, another friend who is a Ukrainian who cares about his mother, bought her an apartment in a new high-rise building. The windows had a beautiful view, and she could enjoy the sunset every day. She had never imagined that a missile would be launched at one of those high-rise apartment buildings. When a nearby apartment building was bombed on the afternoon of February 24th, she had to accept the harsh reality that she would die if she stayed. At first, they fled to western Ukraine, and she is now staying in Germany where her eldest son lives. Unfortunately, their home as an immovable asset has remained in Kyiv.

Since the war, the rent in Kyiv has halved. Real estate agents have been struggling, and construction companies are facing even more problems. There is no prospect of building new houses. The reinforced concrete plants used for construction have been destroyed and the price of concrete has skyrocketed.

The situation in which Ukrainians were forced to leave their homes predates the Chornobyl nuclear accident. During the Russian Revolution at the beginning of the 20th century, wealthy farmers were deprived of their homes. The had to leave their possessions or give them to collective farms in order to survive.

By the time I left for Europe in early February, the mood in Kyiv was already grim. As I packed, I wondered why history had to repeat itself. I could not find the answer to why our neighbors always menaced us when we were free to live on our own land. I still remember that at that moment, some unspoken memory inherited from my ancestors came back to me, and I was struck with fear.

I was leaving just for a few weeks to see friends, but unconsciously, I tucked my PhD diploma into my bag. My grandmother, who became a widow at an early age during World War II, got remarried to a man who had graduated from university before the war but lost his diploma afterwards. When the war ended, the university did not reissue it because there was no proof. The war destroyed the university archive, and there were no records left. So, my grandfather was only able to work at low-paying jobs. Having been told that story since I was a child, I remembered "diploma first".

The Demand for Goods

Ukrainians have a strong belief that "good things last a long time," so they tend to buy the best things for their homes. When going out in public, even in evacuation centers, they avoid dressing sloppily and are as well dressed as possible (I will return to this in the "History of Migration" section). Many Ukrainians who have now taken refuge in Western Europe have noticed a difference in lifestyle. The average middle-class family in Europe generally spend comparatively less money on their homes. They often use mass-market products for wallpaper in their apartments, bathroom, kitchen fixtures, and so on. Ukrainians, after becoming displaced, realized that the standard of living and quality of life in Ukraine is comparatively high.

It seems that the Russian soldiers who invaded Ukraine also noticed the same thing when compared to their own lives. In a telephone conversation overheard by Ukrainian state security officials, one soldier said: "They are living the good life. I could work for 10 years and not be able to afford these home appliances." That is why the soldiers stole washing machines. In a twisted acknowledgement, this may also indicate the high standard of living in Ukraine.

Why do Ukrainians have special feelings toward their homes? Ukrainians have tasted the freedom of capitalism in the 30 years since independence, but they still remember the Soviet era when they could not buy goods freely and that demand for goods remains.

During the socialist era, there was communal housing called *kommunalka*. It was an apartment where several families shared the bathroom, toilet, and kitchen, a step to erase the people's individuality by having them share things and memories. Many "communal things" were established, such as communal farmhouses and cooperatives. According to a friend of mine from East Germany, it was the same story there.

When living in a *kommunalka*, people did not own things, only shared them. They even shared cutlery and dishes. However, everyone in Ukrainian households traditionally had their own spoon, just as in Japanese households. It was a taboo to use someone else's spoon. The custom still exists to put one's spoon in their coffin when they pass away. Thus, even in communal housing, the spoon was the only thing that belonged to the individual. In other words, it may have been the only private property back then.

I assume people affirm safe personal territory by having personal belongings, and so do I. For the first two weeks of the war, I rented the house of a friend who had been away. It was hard for me to accept the fact that I had become a displaced person. The house had everything, but I still wanted something that was my own.

Then one day I went to IKEA in Vienna and bought a couple of spoons and forks, a knife, three plates, and a cup. It was still cold, so I also got a bathrobe, slippers, a blanket and a pillow. My own pillow to see my new dreams. It had been a while since I had spent 100 euros, but I felt like I had gotten a great deal. I put it in my blue bag thinking, "Thank you, IKEA" and returned home. I felt like my friend's house had become a little more like my home.

You understand how much stuff you need for living when you move. I lived in Ukraine, Japan and USA and I have moved about twenty-five times, and I always feel the same about it. About 10 years ago, I bought my own house, which I had dreamed of for a long time. I thought this would finally allow me to settle down. I had no idea that this reality was waiting for me.

What is a Home for Refugees?

When I interviewed displaced Ukrainians in Austria, Germany, Hungary, and the UK. I asked them: "What does home mean to you?" Many of them answered that "it is a place where you have your own things and your own rules." There were also people who said "it is a space where I can live according to my lifestyle."

For Svitlana, who evacuated to Germany with her three children from Kyiv region, making her favorite cup of coffee every morning, just as she did in Kyiv, seems to help her regain her composure. The coffee maker was a gift to her from a German man she had never met before. Misha, her son, plays with a soccer ball that they brought from Kyiv, and his life became the same as before. The lifestyle and feeling there are what they call home.

For my mother, home is the place where she can solve crossword puzzles sitting on the sofa after walking the dog. She was delighted when I gave her a crossword book I bought at Frankfurt airport. I spent three months getting her to learn how to use YouTube, as she wanted to watch the Ukrainian evening news. It was my mother's daily routine at home.

Many European countries have welcomed Ukrainian evacuees. UK people, who know well the meaning of "home," named their program for Ukrainian refugees "Homes for Ukraine". In that program they define home as one's own room, a private space.

I also talked about home with my classmate who never left Kyiv. He never studied abroad, got married early, raised five children, and has been working in Kyiv all his life. He said: "My big home is Ukraine; my smaller home is my house. It is the place where the people I love are waiting for me. It is also "the place where the umbilical cord is buried" (a Ukrainian proverb meaning "the birthplace, one's motherland") and it is our territory. We are not going anywhere. We will stay where our ancestors are buried. And we will fight to the end."

I understand exactly how he feels. I am worried about him, and I send him messages every day. He is now defending our home where our hearts lie.

(June 16, 2022)

3. Conversations with God

Religious Life in Ukraine

When your home is destroyed by an airstrike and you have to escape, who, aside from your family, would you turn to for help? For some, the only other person might be God.

Since the foundation of the Soviet Union in the aftermath of the Russian Revolution, religion was suppressed, churches were destroyed, and people were not allowed to pray freely. The alternative to religion was communism, where people were supposed to believe in the country's leader instead of God. Baptism of newborn children was also forbidden. The only way to have a child baptized was in hiding. Baptizing infants was important because it was felt that the first and greatest means of protecting children in an unstable society was entrusting them to God.

Yet no matter how severe the crackdown on religion and how many churches were closed, Ukrainians remained firm in their faith in God. There were some churches that escaped closure, but they could not be trusted, because the priests there either obeyed the government's authority or secretly reported to their representatives.

Even though people were not going to church, everyone prayed in their homes, and there was always an icon in grandma's house in the countryside. Unlike in the city, no one condemned it there. Some people, even if they were members of the Communist Party in public, still kept the cross they received at their baptism in their desk drawer.

I remember being appalled and crying at home after my Soviet-era primary school class, because my teacher told us that religious people believed that God could cure their children if they got sick, and they would let their children die without seeing a doctor. I was brought up in an environment unfriendly towards religion.

Despite the ban on religion, the Ukrainian people still believed in a higher being that transcended human power. Everyone secretly celebrated Easter and Christmas at home. School teachers knew this. The week before Easter, they would say: "You shall not bring *that* cake for lunch." Teachers knew that during Easter we pupils would be making Easter cakes and *pysankas*[7].

Moreover, it was almost impossible to pray in Ukrainian as the language used in church was Russian. There were only a few churches in Kyiv that held mass in Ukrainian. This was the state policy after the Russian Revolution. Soviet regime closed down most of them in the 1920s and 1930s, when the authorities put fierce pressure on priests and believers. This was notably the case with the churches in Kyiv. Still, Stalin briefly allowed churches to reopen during World War II to generate popular patriotism after the government had promoted "militant atheism". After World War II, the government resumed anti-religious campaigns because it no longer needed the churches to rally support.

After the war started in the eastern part of the country in 2014, many Ukrainians stopped going to churches that held masses in Russian. They did not want to listen to preaching from Moscow because of the politics involved in the mass. They also wanted to talk to God in their own language.

God is Always with You

It was a historical event that the Ukrainian Orthodox Church finally gained independence in 2018. Some argue that it did not become independent on its own, rather because of political pressure. However, the failure of the Church to become independent was also due to politics. Ukraine became an independent country after the Russian Revolution, and the Orthodox Church had an ardent desire for independence. It was not recognized because the Moscow Patriarchate put intense pressure on the Constantinople Patriarchate in Istanbul.

Most Catholic masses were still held in Latin until the 1960s, but after that even Vatican allowed vernacular languages to to be

---

7   Easter egg painted with vibrant colors and patterns—Ukrainian custom for the Easter.

used more commonly in church. If you think about it, if a country is independent, it is common sense for it to have its own religious center and to pray in its native language. It is like paying taxes to your own government instead of to another. This is freedom of mind and spiritual independence.

For a long time, Ukrainians have had a strong rebellious spirit against pressure from above and a tendency to break the mold. In this sense, they were curious about new things and actively tried to communicate with people from different countries and cultures.

Ukrainians who were raised in such circumstances were taught by their parents since childhood that God is in their hearts: God is in your heart wherever you go. You can go to any religious cathedral and pray. You have someone in your heart whom you can talk to at any time and who will protect you. You may call it an angel, a force of nature, or a helping hand, but it is always there near you. That is what original religion was about.

However, this is contrary to the Orthodox Church's way of thinking. According to them, God resides in the Church. It would be fair to say that Ukraine was able to create its own religious world tailored to its difficult historical and political circumstances.

Perhaps, one example is the "home icon" or "family icon," which originated in 17th century Ukraine. Usually, icons were bought at churches but due to their high price, people began to paint icons themselves[8]. Unlike in Greece, Rome, and Russia, the icons were vibrant, and the God depicted on them was not a harsh being who punished people, but someone they could freely consult and be consoled by.

Due to various historical circumstances, Ukrainians have come to speak directly with God without the intervention of churches. This positioning of God may be slightly different from that of common religions.

---

8   A great collection of "home icon" or "family icon" you can find in a Radomyshl castle in Zhytomyr region. https://radozamok.com.ua/about/muse um-of-the-home-icon

Religious Boom Among Young People Immediately after Independence

After Ukraine gained independence in 1991, freedom of religion was recognized. Everyone became interested in religion. According to one of my acquaintances who works for a publishing company, the most popular books printed at that time were suspense novels, business books translated into Ukrainian, and Bibles.

Various religious groups also became active. One of my classmates Natalya wanted to study English but did not have the money to take lessons, so she went to an American denominational church. There was an American there, the first foreigner she had ever seen, and she was able to talk freely with them. Nevertheless, she quit after three months. Her goal was to learn English, not to become religious, although religious organizations at that time were willing to accept students like her.

I was surprised to see many changes around me: a friend of mine who had no interest in religion married a pastor, and my childhood friend's cousin suddenly quit airline school and joined a religious one.

There was, however, also a major incident that drove many young people away from religion. In the fall of 1993, a new religious group called the "White Brotherhood" attempted to die by mass suicide near the St. Sophia Cathedral in Kyiv. The group included many outstanding students from the philosophy and mathematics departments of the Kyiv National University. The police and security service officials detected the situation in advance, arrested the leader and his wife, and brought the students back to their families. However, some of the group members were left with great psychological damage and were unable to return to a normal life. This was widely reported in the media, and everyone realized the negative power of this new religion. Since then, the religious zeal of youth has cooled, and they have come to view religion more soberly.

Religion in Daily Life

The western and central parts of Ukraine have a different attitude toward religion. The further west you go, the more small-sized prayer halls you see, and it is more common for families to go to church together on Sundays. However, this is not the case for Kyiv, a big city in the center of the country. There, religion is more integrated into daily life.

After the New Year, Orthodox Christmas is celebrated on January 7th [9], and on February 15th, the Spring Festival is celebrated from Pagan times. In April, we celebrate Easter, which has little to do with the church, and we also make pysanka (Easter eggs), an ancient symbol of life. On July 7th, we celebrate the Midsummer Festival called Ivana Kupala. That day also coincides with the festival of St. John (a 7-8th century Greek and an important saint in the Orthodox Church).

Another national holiday of Ukraine was recently introduced — the Day of the Baptism of Kyivan Rus is celebrated on July 28th, when Grand Prince of Kyiv was baptized into Christianity in 998. On August 14th and 19th, there are festivals for the honey harvest and apple harvest since ancient times. These also coincide with Christian festivals.

Many people don't go to church on Sundays and don't have icons at home but have small ones in their cars. This is especially true in the case of taxi drivers who usually don't fasten their seatbelts when they drive. It is strange to think that you might not fasten your seatbelt, believing the icons will protect you.

Just as some people believe in God, some Ukrainians believe in the existence of predestination.

Taras Shevchenko, Ukraine's national poet, has a poem about fate. A Japanese friend of mine read it and asked me: "Why does this man resent his fate? How much of one's life is left to fate in the Ukrainian view of life?" That made sense to me, so the next day I asked this question to the students in the class I was

---

9 Since 2022 it's celebrated on 24th of December. So, every holiday started two weeks earlier.

teaching. Some answered 50 percent, some said 80 percent. However, about 90 percent of the students agreed that fate played a key role, perhaps this may be called a culture of superstition. Since people have been through challenging times in history, they have a habit of not boasting too much in public to prevent their luck from escaping. People who believe in God usually do not believe in superstitions, but in Ukraine, faith and superstition peacefully coexist.

My Japanese friend once pointed out to me that in Ukraine people use the word "fate" as an excuse for their passive position. At that time, I thought she was wrong. However, after the war began, I once again started thinking about predestination.

In early March, when I urged one of my friends who had stayed in Kyiv all that time to evacuate, she said: "I will not leave the city. If this is what is destined for me, it can't be helped. Then I will die here." She did not listen to me when I told her to at least try to save her children, if not herself. She was not an action-oriented person to begin with, and it was not surprising that she became catatonic in the midst of war. But I strongly believe that we should not leave people to the "fate of death" even if they have decided so. In the end, I spoke to her husband, and he evacuated the family to the western part of the country: the whole family survived.

Conversations with God Deepened as War Erupted

Since the beginning of the war, Ukrainians have been talking to God in their hearts more often than ever. The same is true for Ukrainians who have fled their homes wearing only their baptismal cross and carrying a few personal belongings. The same is true for Ukrainians who have joined the army. The only help they have is from their own hands, the hands of others, and the hands of God.

In the four months since the war broke out, displaced Ukrainians I met at train stations in Vienna, Budapest, Düsseldorf, and London had crosses around their necks. Many of them also wore red threads on their hands. That red thread is a circle that protects them from demons and has nothing to do with Christianity.

I think if nothing else helps, the thread is fine. This could also be called a superstition, but one could also say that this pagan symbol has become integrated into daily life.

Facing grim times, each Ukrainian is conversing with God. They say: "God, why did it happen? We have done nothing wrong. We were just trying to live happily in our own country. Why didn't you protect us? Why did You put us through this ordeal? But thank you for always being there for us. I am really sorry for telling You this story. But I am telling You this because only You can help me. Please do something about it, God. Unfold an umbrella over us and scoop us out of the fire and into Your palms. I beg You. The elderly, the children, the animals." This is how most of us talk to God every day.

I was watching BBC news reporting on the situation in eastern Ukraine and an old lady in the background was yelling loud, fast prayers as missiles were flying in the air. The British reporter was rolling his eyes wondering why she did not run away.

Here is a story. An acquaintance of mine drove 46 hours with her sons to evacuate to Germany. She was so exhausted in the last hour and a half before arriving that she asked her older son to say a prayer for her, for fear she would doze off while driving. The prayer the boy knew took about 10 minutes, but to prevent his mother from falling asleep, he started his usual conversation with God. He asked God to arrive safely and wished aloud to be protected by God. The family arrived safely. One could say that their prayers were answered, and God protected them.

I am impressed by the fact that they are not just talking, but taking initiative in their actions, too. There is an ancient wisdom expressed in the proverb "You cannot pray to God if you let yourself fall asleep." In other words, God only has your hands. There is also a saying that goes: "God may protect the Cossacks, but they are truly protected by the sword." Would this provide a definition of what God means to the Ukrainians?

(July 14, 2022)

4. A War of Men, Women and Children

A War of Women

Contemplating what a woman on her own could do in the event of war, my friend started going to the gym in the spring of 2014 and concentrated on working out. She thought that women, being physically smaller than men, should be able to protect themselves and their children in peacetime. She later explained to me that her physical training helped her to escape on foot, with her luggage and two young children in February 2022.

During wartime, women, in particular, are in mortal danger and need to evacuate. Once they are evacuated, they need to rebuild a new life. In the process, they must overcome anxiety and other mental health issues, as well as all kinds of dangerous situations. I thought my friend's story was unusual when I heard it in the spring of 2014, however, I often recalled it during the winter of 2022. I regretted that during the two years of the COVID-19 pandemic I had spent so much time researching and writing and so little time going to the gym.

A friend of mine, a Japanese woman working as a reporter who went to Kyiv in August, once asked me the same question: "What can one woman do when war breaks out?" I stumbled over an answer. It is true that in a war, women will feel twice as much danger as men. Merely passing near a group of strange men is enough to make one shiver.

Yet when you are scared, conversely, it can give you extra courage. In the past six months, many different women have so impressed me. A mother in her 40s who drove herself and her family to evacuate to Germany. A single woman in her 30s who returned to Ukraine from the UK, where she was studying, took her bedridden mother back with her. A businesswoman in her 50s who collects donations for the army. A former maths teacher in her 80s who makes military camouflage nets. A successful psychologist in her 40s who provides counseling on a voluntary basis. Many women have enlisted in the army. Students and office workers have become nurses, drivers, and military spokespeople, and are working hard for a Ukrainian victory. One recent poster I saw on the streets of Kyiv shows a woman in military uniform with the slogan "There is no weaker sex in Ukraine."

There may be women who are physically weaker but sometimes mentally stronger than men. Looking back on the 20th century, when many Ukrainian men were killed during the Russian revolution and civil wars, the great famine, WWII and Stalin's purges, everyone has learned to survive and make a living for themselves, even single women. After 30 years of independence, we had finally come to a society where we do not have to think about such things, where we can all feel safe and where there are men to protect women. This is when the war began.

My friend Katya was a busy businesswoman working for a foreign company, but when the war broke out, she stayed in Kyiv with her husband and son instead of evacuating. When I asked her why she did not leave even though she had arranged train tickets, she replied that her husband was mentally fragile by nature and might become depressed if left alone. She said optimistically: "The war will be over soon," but 8 months later she is still in Kyiv[10].

Certainly, not all women are strong. During wars, it is quite common for women to be sexually victimized simply because they are women. There was a sign on the state border from Slovenia into Austria that read, "Please signal if you are a target of human trafficking," on a background of yellow and blue Ukrainian colors. It made sense to me. Victims may not be able to say it directly, but they can give a sign to the border officials. A friend of mine who evacuated to the UK told me that there was a similar question on the entry questionnaire. She also told me that she was also given emergency contact information. This was to prevent so-called "modern slavery." This is certainly necessary. Over the past 8 months, I have

---

10 In May of 2024 her so called "fragile" husband decided to enroll to the army and now fighting at the eastern front. Katya is still in Kyiv with her 12-year-old son.

seen many displaced women working in the kitchens of hotels and restaurants in Europe for less pay than the locals.

A War of the Men

Valya, a nurse at the surgery department, who had been in the hospital for more than 70 days and nights since the war began was asked: "Why didn't you evacuate?" She replied: "I stayed because I was needed here. It is more rational to stay here than to do nothing and be mentally cornered in the evacuation center." This sentiment is understandable.

I heard the exact same story from Vitaliy, a taxi driver in his 60s in Poland. In addition to working for a company in Kyiv, he was also managing 2 parking lots in the center of town and was extremely busy. He had taken refuge with his family at his younger daughter's place in Poland, where she was attending university. He felt he would go crazy if he stayed at home all the time, so he took up taxi driving.

Men are also going through a great deal of hardship in war. Not everyone is necessarily capable of fighting. It is also hard for families that have been torn apart by war. It has been a time of tough choices, especially for men. They are deeply concerned about whether to join the army or not, and then what they can do for the army. Since February 24th, while a fair number of sons of rich families have been able to leave Ukraine, ordinary men between the ages of eighteen and sixty have not been able to leave the country. Everyone is preparing to be called up by the army.

Every man who stays in the country feels the pressure of duty. A male friend of mine asked me: "Have you noticed that not a single male politician has smiled in the last eight months?" Indeed, they have not. These are not times to smile about.

Men who enlisted in the military have it tough. Their military service is for an indefinite period, with no prospect of coming home until the war is over. According to the most recent legislation, only fathers with a third child born after they have enlisted in the military can return to their families. Two writers who had been also drafted in 2014 petitioned the President for that "indefinite" amendment.

Those who have not yet been drafted are doing their best to be useful in other ways. One of my friends, a historian who has loved orienteering[11] since he was young, is one of them. He is from Poltava, a city halfway between Kyiv and Kharkiv in the northeast. After sending his family back to Poland, he returned to his hometown to give lessons on "map reading", so that people could evacuate if their smartphones were out of service.

When I suggested: "Why don't you make an online course on YouTube?" he replied: "No, I cannot. The terrain around our area is very unusual, and I should not let the enemy know our peculiarities. I only do offline face-to-face classes." These are indeed such times. Unlike in peacetime, the map itself has become an important piece of information.

Also, it seems to me that Ukrainian men, started to express their feelings during the war. When seeing their families off at the train station, they shed tears. When they return home after evacuating their families, they cannot sleep alone and stay up late at night sewing balaclavas for the army, as my friend Ihor did. One of my students told me that when a missile was launched at Kyiv this month, there was an old man among the people gathered at the subway station who was crying. He must have seen the damage done to the office building near the Kyiv station and felt he could not forgive it.

A War of the Children

Children can adjust and cope with changes in their environment. They are the first to make friends in evacuation centers. However, they experience hardships too.

When I look at children's drawings made after the war started, I can see their feelings about the war, which they cannot easily express. When my eleven-year-old nephew showed me a

---

11 A sport where participants use a map and compass to navigate through unfamiliar areas, moving quickly to reach specific locations.

drawing he had made in his first art class after taking refuge in Austria, I was perplexed. The first assignment was to sketch his hand and use that to draw something over. At first glance, it looked like a colorful bird painted on a black background. However, upon closer inspection, the hand/bird looked as if it was screaming or calling for help. When I asked him if he was scared of the evacuation, he replied with a blank expression: "Not really." Yet everything in that painting looked scary to me. In his other paintings, there often were tanks, weapons, soldiers, and the Ukrainian flag. I wish all young Ukrainian children who have been through frightening experiences could be protected. And they could draw only peaceful things.

Fathers often come up to the border with their wives and children when seeing them out of the country. Saying goodbye at the border becomes another painful story. Small children cry. "I don't want to let go of my daddy." My eleven-year-old nephew hugged the border official and begged with tears in his eyes: "Uncle, please let my daddy through." The official was cold. He turned to his mother and said: "Madam, move your child away."

Smaller children do not understand the situation, so they assume that their father does not want to go with them. My friend's five-year-old boy, who was evacuated to Hungary, did not want to answer the phone calls coming from his dad. When they asked him about it, he replied: "Dad left us and I don't want to talk to him," to everyone's surprise. What was going on in that tiny head was a mystery.

When the war started, the seven-year-old son of my friend, who was hiding in a basement in Kyiv region, could not understand why the war was happening, so asked: "Why does Putin hate us?" Indeed, why? I do not have the answer. Perhaps, he wanted the territory of Ukraine, but not the Ukrainians living there.

War has intruded not only into the reality and dreams of children, but also their games. Ukrainian children used to gather in large numbers in front of their houses to play, an activity that is now disappearing. The other day, however, my friend Oleksiy was going home, and his car was stopped by a group of children between the ages of 7 and 10 at the house entrance. Apparently, they were playing a war game called "Checkpoint" and even though the kids knew my friend, they properly checked if he was a resident of the house. Both sides laughed and the kids let him through, but he said afterwards: "The war has changed children's games…" It is true.

Women, men, children… Everyone is defending themselves, hating this war brought in by Russia, and praying for the future of Ukraine. We hate war, but we must fight. Because if we do not fight, Ukraine as a country and the Ukrainian people will no longer exist.

I would like to quote a poem by the Italian writer Gianni Rodari.

> There are things to be done every day:
> washing oneself, studying, playing,
> setting the table
> at midday.
> There are things to be done every night:
> closing one's eyes, sleeping,
> having dreams to dream,
> ears for listening.
> There are things never to be done,
> neither by day nor by night,
> neither by sea nor by land:
> for example, war[12].

(October 27, 2022)

---

12 Translation by the author

5. The War and Smartphones

Finding it Hard to Relax: The Compulsion to Check the News

Since the pandemic, the amount of time spent using smartphones and computers has increased. The screen time of Ukrainian children and students also saw a sharp increase through online classes. Some of my students got tired of online classes for their master's degree programs. Additionally, the worsening economic situation caused financial worries and some of them decided not to apply for doctoral programs. It was a great pity. In general, Ukrainians have better eyesight than people from Japan and other countries that use Chinese characters. However, during the COVID-19 outbreak, both adult and children's eyesight worsened and those wearing glasses increased.

Since the beginning of the war, screentime spent on smartphones has doubled again. Children, adults, and the elderly wake up every morning, and fearfully check the news lying in bed. They reply to the messages of relatives and friends, checking the chat groups of neighbors in Kyiv, and only then get up and wash their faces. The procedure is the same when they go to bed and many times during the day.

I have been hearing similar stories from Ukrainians of different professions and different countries over the past 7 months. They cannot calm down without checking the news on their phones. Is their country, the capital Kyiv, still there, or have missiles destroyed them? Checking the news became an important part of people's lives. It brings temporary relief. It is understandable. Though one cannot affect anything by oneself, one can at least read the news every day.

Surely, it may be a waste of time, and passively receiving scary information only adds to the stress. Before the COVID-19 pandemic, one of my friends limited his children's time online to 30 minutes a day. Instead, they played table games together, drew pictures, and focused on studying math. He wanted to raise them as future content creators, not content consumers, and while they are on their phones, they cannot do anything else. They cannot create.

Seniors Embracing Smartphone Technology

In any case, screentime has increased. However, it is difficult to quit using a smartphone. Unlike the days of landline phones, there is no need to remember phone numbers. Everything is kept in phone memory. Contacts of family members and friends, banks, post offices, maps, pedometers, weather reports, as well as books to read, language-learning applications, gas station membership cards, and even Instagram, Twitter, Zoom, and Facebook to keep a finger on the pulse of current events. The phone even has applications for taxis and shopping.

In Ukraine, in the two years of the pandemic, all important documents—passport, driver's license, insurance and vaccine certificates—have been digitalized and brought together in one smartphone application call Diya[13]. The smartphone is life itself. Some people did not want to go digital because they thought their personal information would be stolen, but they became grateful after the war. Even those who have evacuated can check, show and submit all the necessary documents without having them in physical form.

Digitalization has advanced in other areas as well. It is now convenient to register marriages, divorces, and even births online or through apps, without having to wait in line at government offices.

As digitization progressed, the elderly had no choice but to follow this trend. The first challenge for them was the COVID-19 vaccination. Reservations for the shots were made online, and in the beginning, young people were helping them. But then the war broke out, and even the elderly became proficient in using smartphones.

---

13   Means "action" in Ukrainian.

Seventy and eighty-year-old senior women, who previously were not good with technology and IT and only used the phone function on their smartphones, began watching Ukrainian news on YouTube in a foreign country where they had taken refuge. Ukraine's state-run TV station also broadcasts news online for 24 hours a day. Previously, seniors did not even want to use the TV remote control, and this change and growth is unbelievable.

They are now able to send their cheerful faces to their families. When I first received a photo from my mother, I thought for a moment that somebody had stolen her phone. I immediately called her and was relieved to find out that it was she who sent the photo, and that she could learn things quickly if needed or if her life was in danger.

They can learn even faster when they have young people around. Since the war started, more senior people are starting to use new media like TikTok and Instagram thanks to their children and grandchildren.

One example is Yaroslava Mykolaivna, a famous eighty-four-year-old grandmother in Ukraine. Her granddaughter created an account for her on Instagram and Tik Tok and are helping her to publish something every day[14]. This has made her a beloved grandma all over Ukraine. Melania has lived in a village near the Polish border ever since she was born. She experienced war as a child, but never thought it would come again. Feeling she was too old to do anything, she started to bring in generous portions of homemade dumplings for the soldiers and sent out messages on social media every day. She introduces her viewers to housework, yard work, and daily life. She has become a beloved figure, followed by people in their 30s, 40s, and even 50s who have lost their grandmothers or did not have kind grandmothers. Now she has 827,000 followers on TikTok.

---

14   https://www.tiktok.com/@melania.movvie

Connecting Through Social Networks

Nowadays, thanks to social networks, we have become globalized in both good and bad ways, and it is becoming harder to hide information. As long as you have the internet, you can disseminate information wherever you are. Moreover, unlike Facebook or Instagram, Tik-Tok can deliver a message to many people in no time. People sitting in basements due to air raid warnings, military servicemembers, refugees, and people living in distant foreign countries are all connected by one invisible thread.

Since the beginning of the war, a new trend has emerged in social networking. Military personnel, who previously have rarely sent out messages, are now as active as politicians. Thanks to Starlink, a satellite system operated by Elon Musk's SpaceX, soldiers fighting in the east have access to the internet all the time and are connected to their families.

Besides the usual postings, Ukrainian songs are also performed for a global audience. Many soldiers are singing, dancing and making fun of the enemy. People can have access now not only to entertainment, but also to essential information. When the Zaporizhzhia nuclear power plant was attacked in March of 2022, one civilian streamer broadcast the footage to the world, which attracted a lot of attention.

After the Russian invasion started, Ukrainians began to exchange information in various chat groups. People started to make more connections with neighbors whom they did not even know before. In my apartment building chat group with neighbors in Kyiv the exchange of information is going on every day. At the end of February, right after the war started, high-rise apartment buildings were targeted by enemy air strikes, so the residents of the apartment building locked the door to the rooftop and shared an hourly duty to checked it. The entrance to the rooftop was sprinkled with flour so if anyone walked upon it the residents would know. I wondered if they learned this method from suspense novels. Moreover, when the rumor spread that green and blue lights on windows would make the building a target for air strikes, residents were checking all the windows in their buildings to see if any apartment had such colored lights. Everyone was trying hard, but sometimes people got it wrong. Once, there was a bit of a commotion during a blackout when a green nightlight in a child's room at one of the flats turned on automatically. The owners were away, so the neighbors had to enter the apartment, only to discover that everything was fine. This time, in the end, all's well that ends well.

On other occasions it did not end so well. One day in May, someone sent a message to that chat which said: "I hear a woman screaming on the ninth floor." Since there were only five families living in the building, where two hundred families had been living pre-war, everyone wanted to know what was happening, so they called the police. The police officer duly arrived but had to leave since there were no more screams. Two hours later, a message came to the chat from the person who had screamed, saying: "I am sorry for the disturbance. I got a call that all my family in Mariupol were killed, and I couldn't contain my feelings..." Just reading that made my heart skip a beat. I was confused and did not know how to respond.

Since the war broke out, well-known Ukrainian journalist Andriy Tsaplienko has created a Telegram channel, where various information is shared faster than in the newspapers. Besides that, every day I check the chat group with my classmates (how are they?) and chat groups of my apartment building (are they intact?). It takes me a lot of time just to read what is new in these chats, which keeps me busy every day. In any case, for the past 8 months, the information I received from social media and channels on my smartphone was faster than from newspapers and TV.

Writing all this reminded me of one more thing from the past. Once when I was a child my grand aunt showed me that every time she came to Kyiv from the countryside, she always had a note in her pocket with the destination address. In case she ever got lost in the big city, she would ask someone to get her to that address. I heard that this practice became widespread after some children were separated from their parents during World War II, but I never thought those days would come again. I recalled this when I was watching the news. There was footage of a child being sent to an evacuation center with his parents' cell phone numbers written on his back with a red pen. It was heartbreaking.

The Danger of Smart Phones

War has shown us that a smartphone can easily turn from something that saves us to something that puts us in danger. If you check the recorded information and photos, you can find out everything about a person's past and present.

Apparently, when people from the Russian-occupied territories were returning to Ukraine, their smartphones were checked in many ways. People who had phones with the only function to make calls were able to return home rather smoothly, whereas in many cases people with smartphones were in danger as their phones were checked for the information stored on them, especially if they had pictures of the Ukrainian flag, national dress, or photos taken with military personnel.

The use of smartphones is different in times of peace compared to wartime, which means that information that was previously considered normal to post in a chat may become dangerous. For example, posting a photo on Twitter or Instagram becomes extremely dangerous as the photo file contains location information and the exact place can be easily identified. I also heard that a smartphone carries radio waves, which can easily reveal your location.

To prevent smartphones from turning from friend to foe, Ukrainian media has recently been making education campaigns for civilians about smartphone usage during war.

(October 7, 2022)

II. A Country Called Ukraine

1. The Closest Country: Poland

Poland Seen from Ukraine

Apart from Russia and Belarus, Ukraine shares borders with Poland, Slovakia, Romania, Hungary and Moldova. After the Russian invasion, the response of these neighboring countries was very prompt. Poland, in particular, was highly active and provided a lot of support, for which all Ukrainians are incredibly grateful.

When I think of Poland, I think of the travel and history novels I read as a child, such as Alfred Szklarski's work about the adventures of Tomek, and Henryk Sienkiewicz's "With Fire and Sword," about the Poles who fought the Ukrainian Cossacks[15] in the 17th century. Also "The Double Life of Veronique," which I saw as a student. I was also impressed by Krzysztof Kieslowski's film trilogy "Three colors" — "Blue," "White," "Red."

Since our countries border each other, there were times when we were close and times when we were not. There were times when parts of Ukraine were Polish territory and when Cossacks were hired to work for the Polish king. There were times when we had mixed feelings and did not trust each other. It was not an easy relationship from a historical point of view, but cultural exchanges have been going on for a long time. Since the Middle Ages, various cultures, cultural relics, and knowledge from the West have entered Ukraine via Poland. For example, Cossacks supported establishing of the first Orthodox school for their children, the Mohyla Academy, which was modeled after the schools in Poland run by Catholic religious orders and churches.

During the Cold War, the trains between Kyiv and Warsaw brought many things. The Beatles and rock music, which had a major influence on Ukrainian people in the 60s and 70s, jeans and vinyl records, came in via Poland. In the 1970s and 1980s, the

---

15 Cossacks originate from people who fled serfdom and formed settlements in remote areas, these self-governing groups became skilled in arms and horsemanship.

Sopot Music Festival in Poland was often aired on Ukrainian television. Popular music of the time came via Poland. I remember the taste of Fanta, a unique "foreign drink", which my brother-in-law who worked at the railway brought from one of his trips to Germany and Poland in 1980s.

Polish influence was also political. In the 1980s, the successful example of the Solidarity movement for democracy in Poland inspired the *Narodny Rukh Ukrainy* (means *People's Movement of Ukraine*), a civil movement that later fought for Ukraine's independence.

When the Soviet Union collapsed, the Ukrainian economy was in a difficult situation with skyrocketing prices and shortages of goods, and many people took buses to get to the markets of Poland to sell cameras, Soviet-made electrical goods, and other items. They also bought clothes to sell them at Ukrainian markets to make a living. Poland was quick to leave socialism, achieved economic growth, and became richer than Ukraine. This appeal has made the Polish language popular, especially over the past 15 years. Many schools have established Polish language departments and the number of students from Ukraine studying in Poland has increased.

Before the modern era, Poland was a large kingdom, and much of Ukraine was part of its territory at one time. Historically, Poles sometimes had a superiority complex about Ukraine. However, there were many instances of cooperation between Ukrainians and Poles at contrasting times and places. One example was in distant Manchuria in the 1930s. There, Ukrainians and Poles, who had been displaced by World War I and the Russian Revolution, fought hand in hand as ethnic minorities and formed a regional division of the organization called Prometheus[16], which wished to dissolve the Soviet Union from within and give independence to all minorities.

---

16 Prometheism was initially a Polish political initiative, developed by Józef Piłsudski between 1904 and 1939. Its goal was to support oppressed nations within the Russian Empire, and later the Soviet Union, in their pursuit of independence and eventually deconstruct empires from within.

Poland as a Place to Settle

A study based on public opinion polls in Poland shows that until the Orange Revolution of 2004[17] feelings toward Ukraine varied. For example, the mass murder of Poles in Volhynia region during World War II and the increase of migrant workers such as helpers, babysitters, and construction workers from Ukraine in the 1990s, when the economy was in decline, had a negative impact on Ukraine's image. However, many of the responses at that time were that they could not distinguish between Russians, Ukrainians, and Belarusians. They were all considered "Russians" by the Poles.

Ukraine was part of the USSR while Poland had a long history of independence. As they transitioned from socialism, many Poles went to Germany, France, and the UK in search of jobs. Similarly, for the first 10 years or so after Ukraine became independent, Ukrainians often went to Poland as migrant workers.

As the economic situation in both countries gradually improved, relations between the two countries grew stronger, and they sometimes co-hosted cultural events. Co-hosting of the UEFA championship in 2012 brought Ukraine and Poland closer. Tourism has flourished as it has become easier to travel between the two countries, and the number of Polish tourists in Ukraine has increased. With tourism on the rise, there were many more opportunities to learn about the country, which led to mutual understanding.

After the war broke out in Eastern Ukraine in 2014, many people moved to Poland in search of safety. Since there was a period of a living as one country, many people, especially in western Ukraine, have mixed ancestry, for instance, a grandfather who was Polish. If they can prove that they have Polish roots, they can obtain a Polish residence permit.

---

17 Period when the ruling party candidate Viktor Yanukovych won the presidential election, but revelations of electoral fraud on the part of the ruling party led to massive protests and a redo election resulted in the victory of opposition candidate Viktor Yushchenko.

This was especially attractive to university students. After graduating from a Polish university, they could work anywhere in Europe. The tuition fees were almost the same as in Ukraine, yet there were many more possibilities. Considering their children's future, quite often parents opted for Polish universities. The daughter of my childhood friend studied international relations in Warsaw and then went on to study in the United States. The cost of living in Poland is a bit higher than in Ukraine, yet the salaries are higher, atmosphere is safer, and there is a lot of quality food. Some of my other students studied a little at Ukrainian universities, then moved to Polish universities, graduated, and got jobs in Polish consulting firms, schools and museums.

Some people consider Poland as a place to settle for the safety and future of their families. A female friend of mine, a businesswoman living in Lviv, sold her three businesses in Ukraine in 2014 and moved to Poland. People around her thought she was thinking about expanding her business and providing an education for her only daughter, but in fact she had other reasons. She was worried that, since the war had broken out in the east, her beloved husband who was working as psychiatrist might be mobilized to the army. Within 6 years of the COVID-19 outbreak, she had reopened her own businesses in Poland and Slovakia, and her husband runs a private practice.

In Poland, if you call a taxi in Warsaw or in southern city of Krakow, the driver is often Ukrainian. When I talk to them, I can learn about modern Poland and the migration of Ukrainians to Poland.

Ivan, a driver in Krakow, is from Lviv region, he studied and lived in Kharkiv for 8 years before deciding to move to Poland in 2014. His sole reason was that running a private company is easier — no bribes are required when applying, and as long as you pay your taxes properly, there will be no problems.

Roman, who is attending law school in Poland, moved to Warsaw 4 years ago for the same reason. Petro, a truck driver, had a similar reason. He believes that hard work can help him to support his family and build a stable future. Olena, an actor who works on stage and in movies, also said that the situation in

Poland is better than in Ukraine for freelance artists. One of my students, who graduated from the history department of the National University of Kyiv Mohyla Academy, studied at a Polish graduate school, got his PhD, and is now teaching at a Polish university. He says that unlike in Ukraine, he can make a living only on his university salary. The people I have mentioned so far had already moved to Poland before the Russian invasion.

After the Full-scale Invasion

After the Russian invasion began on February 24th, 2022, Poland opened its borders and became a place of sanctuary for Ukrainians. Having experienced occupation by Nazi Germany and the Soviet Union in the fall of 1939, Poland was deeply sympathetic toward Ukraine. I was touched to see pictures of Ukrainians gathered in big crowds at the Polish border, and of Poles handing out tea and buns at the train station in the freezing cold, to Ukrainians who received them with tears in their eyes. My friend was also impressed by the kindness of the Polish volunteers who helped her sick mother from Kharkiv.

Shelters have been built in Warsaw and several other cities, where many Ukrainians are still living with the hope of returning home. Many Ukrainians have found jobs and are working hard. One of examples is the Marriott Hotel near Warsaw train station, where more than half of the customer service staff are young Ukrainians. Many Ukrainian women were also cooks at hotels in Warsaw and Krakow. When I said "dziękuję" (thank you in Polish), they responded "dyakuyu" (thank you in Ukrainian). Other examples are people working as staff at beauty salons, nail salons, and cashiers at convenience stores. Many of the displaced people decided not to receive the single living allowance support provided by the Polish government, but instead managed to quickly find work and live off their savings.

More than 5 million Ukrainians have moved to Poland since the invasion began. According to statistics from the summer of 2021, previously there were about 1.5 million migrant workers. This is a striking number because of the sheer scale.

No one expected that the historically complicated relations between the two countries would improve in the wake of this great misfortune. For Poland, Ukraine has changed from an "unfamiliar neighbor" to a country that they vaguely understand. Interest in the language and culture has also increased.

The abovementioned actress Olena also gives private Ukrainian lessons to three Polish students. They are people in their 30ss and 40ss, a newspaper reporter, a researcher, and a businessman. Until now, younger Poles had thought that Ukrainians, Russians, and Belarusians were all "Russians," but they found out that this was not true and were surprised at the similarity of the languages of both countries. One can speak Ukrainian at the cashier in Polish supermarkets and still be able to shop as usual.

Many Ukrainians fled with little or nothing, so they need to do a little shopping. Thus, it could be said that their consumption contributes the Polish economy. Moreover, many of the Kyiv offices of foreign companies relocated to Warsaw. Surely, the rent of the offices became higher, and the salary level though it was originally high, has been adjusted to the Polish standard of living.

Ukrainians who fled the country spend more money on experience-oriented things than on material goods. After escaping with their lives from the Russian invasion, people reevaluated family ties and are taking more opportunities for family vacations. Having left all their belongings behind in Ukraine, they are convinced they should collect happy memories instead of things. The hearts of those who have fled the war cannot be healed with things. But it can be healed through the quality time with their dear ones.

Polish politicians also visited Ukraine several times during the past eight months. In May of 2022, President Andrzej Duda began his speech in the Ukrainian Parliament with the words in Ukrainian: "Greetings, brothers and sisters of Ukraine." He then continued: "I would like to let you know that your loved ones: spouses, parents, children, grandchildren, those millions of people who had to leave Ukraine, fleeing the tragedy of war, also to Poland—are not refugees in our country. They are our guests.

I assure you that they are safe in Polish homes while you are fighting with such bravery to defend your country's independence".

It was heartwarming to hear him say this. The city of Rzeszów, on the border, became known as "the city that saved the Ukrainians," as many Ukrainians were able to evacuate through there.

If you compare Warsaw with Kyiv or Kraków with Lviv, they have similarities. Warsaw was almost totally destroyed in the war, so much of the architecture is new, whereas Krakow was largely spared. Krakow and Lviv are the most similar because of the Habsburg roots, whereas Warsaw and Kyiv have old towns but really expanded post-1945. There is a lot of greenery in the cities also, so it may be easy to get used to them. The Polish people are truly warm and welcoming. Of course, some people may be dissatisfied with an influx of foreigners. Such people are everywhere. They may claim that the war made gas and electricity bills higher. The war indeed has had a huge economic and psychological impact on Europe. However, Ukrainians whose lives were saved and who would remember the warm reception by Poland for the rest of their lives, will develop even better relations between both countries in the future.

On November 15th, 2 people were killed when a misfired missile fell on a Polish village near the border. It was heartbreaking to hear the news. I think about Ukraine and Poland all the time.

(November 18, 2022)

2. The Two Seas of Ukraine

The Origins of the Black Sea

In Japan, there is a holiday called "Sea Day" in July, just as one would expect from a country surrounded by the sea. The fact that Ukraine has two seas, the Black Sea and the Sea of Azov, may not be well known to many people. My Japanese friends often ask me, "Is the Black Sea really black?" as well as about the origin of the name and my thoughts regarding the Black Sea.

The Black Sea has had different names depending on the period. It was known to the Greeks from the 8th century BC since they expanded their trading roots and colonies. The philosopher Seneca called it "the Scythian Sea." Herodotus in his "History" called it "the Northern Sea."

According to the geographer and historian Strabo, this sea was named "the Black Sea" by Greek settlers. There were storms and fog occurring on the sea, making it difficult for marine traffic, and the coast was unknown and uncivilized, inhabited by hostile Scythians and Tauri. The Greeks gave the sea a fitting name "the Inhospitable Sea" or "the Black Sea." After they settled in the area from the 6th century B.C., it became "the Hospitable Sea". They probably befriended the sea.

Meanwhile, in the ancient Russian Primary Chronicle written in the 12th century, it was called the "Sea of the Kyiv (Rus)". There are various theories about the origin of the name "Black Sea". Some say that it is derived from the Turkish language, where it is called "Karadeniz/Black Sea". Turkic peoples had a tradition of indicating direction by color, and black meant north. Thus, "the Black Sea" means the northern sea. Some people still use that name. By the way, the color for the south is white in Turkish, and the Mediterranean Sea is called "the White Sea" (Akdeniz). However, it is not clear whether the influence of Turkey is the reason the name "Black Sea" became widespread.

The Black Sea washes the coasts of Ukraine, Romania, Bulgaria, Russia, Turkey and Georgia. The maximum depth is

2210 meters, and the total area is 422,000 square kilometers. Besides, the water at depths of 150 to 200 meters is high in hydrogen sulfide, and in some cases may catch fire. After sailing through these waters, sailors noticed that the anchors and other metal parts of their ships turned black and called the sea "Black." In the Black Sea, the main current flows counterclockwise along the coast, and two tributaries join in the middle of the sea, twisting from north to south. In the 19th century, the crews of British ships sailed on the current from Odesa to Istanbul without raising their sails. On the seabed, there are mussels, oysters, and shellfish brought by ships from the Far East. The sea is rising at a rate of 20 to 25 centimeters every 100 years.

Joseph Pitton de Tournefort, a botanist of the reign of Louis XIV of France, said: "Whatever the ancients said, there is nothing black in the Black Sea." Furthermore, there is a popular song from the Soviet era with the lyrics "The Black Sea, bluest in the world." There is also a soccer club From Odesa called "Chornomorets" (Black Sea People).

Before World War II, a special political concept was born in Ukraine, different from "continental politics", and considered a maritime view. It was the "Black Sea Doctrine" proposed by Yuriy Lypa, originally from Odesa, who was a doctor, political critic, and poet. According to this theory, the states around the Black Sea should form a political bloc and its leader should be Ukraine. It says that *"the Black Sea is the economic and spiritual foundation for the states in the vicinity. For Ukraine, the Black Sea is a vital space. And considering its area, resources and human energy, Ukraine should be the first among the countries around the Black Sea to make clever use of the sea. Therefore, the "Black Sea Doctrine" should be a priority in Ukraine's foreign policy."*

Another Sea, Sea of Azov

The Sea of Azov, another sea of Ukraine, is the smallest and most inland of the 63 seas in the world. It is also called "the sea for children" in Ukraine. The Sea of Azov is the shallowest in the world, with a maximum depth of 13.5 meters. In summer, the temperature of the sea is about 28-30 degrees Celsius. The ancient Greeks did not consider it a sea, but called it "Maeotian Lake", the Romans called it the "Maeotian Marshes", the Scythians "Karachulak" (full of fish) Sea, and the Arabs "Pontus Sea" or "Black Sea". Today, the Turkish also call it "Azak Benizi" and it means "The Sea by Azak" (an old name for the city of Azov).

In the Slavic historical records, this sea was first named Azov in 1389, but the name itself probably emerged a century or two earlier. There is a theory that the name of the sea originated from the city of Azov. Azov was a colony of the Bosporus Kingdom in the Greek period, the Principality of Tmutarakan in the 10th-12th century and became a part of the Ulus of Jochi (Kipchak Khanate or the Golden Horde Khanate) in the 13th century, and then the Crimean Khanate (vassals of the Ottoman Empire) in the 14th century. The Cossacks were fighting here in 1695-1696. There is a Ukrainian Cossack folk song about three Cossack brothers who fled from Turkish arrest in the town of Azov.

In the 18th century, this area was ceded to the Russian Empire following the Russo-Turkish War. By the way, the Turkish word "azan" means "the one below" and the Cherkess word "uzev" means "mouth of the river" or "estuary." In Ukrainian sources, the names Azov and Ozov were both used. The early Soviet map of 1929 shows the Ukrainian name of the Sea of Ozov.

Since the 17th century the Sea of Azov has been the theater of many military conflicts, including the Crimean War (1853-1856), a full-scale war with the participation of the British and French against the Russian army.

The Sea of Azov is not deep, but because of that is very much loved by parents with small children. It is safer compared to the Black Sea. The narrow Kerch Strait, at most about 4 kilometers long, connects the Black Sea and separates the Kerch Peninsula. In the middle of the strait is the island of Tuzla, which belongs to Ukraine. Until 1925, it was a small peninsula, but a storm collapsed the connecting land, and it became an island. Therefore, Ukraine got a territory of 6.5 kilometers long and 500 meters wide[18]. In addition, there is a Syvash lake called "The Rotten Sea," and a fair number of sanatoriums for long-term treatment of tuberculosis and other diseases that use the mud for treatment have been built there.

It is a pity that foreigners and especially Japanese people, who have a special affection for the sea, do not know that Ukraine, a flat country with few mountains, has two seas, which have had a major influence not only on the geography of the country, but also on its history.

(July 31, 2022)

---

18 In 2003, Russia attempted to assert control over this island by constructing a dam, leading to a territorial dispute with Ukraine. As a result, Ukraine regained control and established a border guard presence there. Following the occupation of Crimea in 2014, the Russian government constructed the Kerch Bridge over the Kerch Strait, opening it in 2018-2019 to link mainland Russia with Crimea by both road and rail.

3. The Trauma of Ukrainian People

Historical Trauma

My grandmother used to say to me: "[Everything is fine] as long as there is no war." However, I naively believed in peace, so I thought: "Of course, there will be no war. Are you serious?" I believed that war was something far away, something that had nothing to do with me.

More than 6 months have passed since the war broke out. When the war started in February, everyone expected that it would be over by summer. A historian friend of mine told me around April that it might be just like World War II when everyone thought it would be over by Christmas (in fact, it lasted six years), and I thought: "Of course, it might not. Are you serious?"

What is the trauma of World War II for Ukrainians? There are many things. First, the Germans invaded Kyiv and the city was occupied for more than 2 years. Many people lost their fathers and homes in the war, and the remaining families were taken to Germany as cheap labor. Even the fertile Ukrainian soil was taken to Germany by railway. Many people, including Jews, were killed in Kyiv. More than 700 towns and 28,000 villages were completely destroyed in the course of World War II.

The death of Ukrainians exceeded 6 million people and the civilian casualties were much higher than military ones in Ukraine. After the war, a generation suffered from a lack of marriage partners, and many other problems.

The older generation feels reluctant to speak German because of the long occupation by Germany. Postwar Soviet war movies also created a exaggerated image of Germans. In the movies, only specific German words such as "stop," "hands up," "hurry up," "give me some milk and eggs," etc. were shown. Every child in the Soviet era knew German to that extent. When I traveled in Germany as a student, I once froze when a police officer asked me to show him my passport at a train station. I did not know what to do, laugh or cry. Nowadays, some Ukrainian refugees living in Germany have returned to Ukraine after 6 months, having failed to get used to the language, lifestyle and strict rules.

Ukrainians have many traumatic experiences. After declaring the brief independence of the Ukrainian People's Republic in 1918, Ukrainians suffered from a lack of independence. Further suffering followed: the man-made famine of 1932-33 (Holodomor), widows losing their husbands in World War II, children growing up without their fathers, the damage caused by the accident at the Chornobyl nuclear power plant. Finally, there are people who became refugees in the current war, as well as massacres that happened in Irpin and Bucha. One can only imagine what a terrible fate it must have been. The superstition that no matter how hard one tries, some extra force will always get in the way, has naturally emerged in Ukraine due to the historical environment. There is a Ukrainian saying: "The only help you can give is to leave me alone."

Collective and Family Memories

In Ukraine, the thought and motivation for business is different between regions that experienced famine and those that did not. After all, national, regional, and individual experiences are connected. The times when people were pressured and could not decide their own destiny became a trauma and a collective memory. Even though I was born decades after the famine and did not experience it directly, it still bothers me to see my grandmother eating breadcrumbs left on the table whilst cleaning it.

As a researcher, I approach many things academically, but I realized that when the time comes, the historical traumas that have been ingrained in my body surface and influence my behavior.

The first such experience was in March 2020. I was in the USA when the world was busy dealing with the COVID-19 outbreak. I went to the local supermarket to buy some food, but when I looked at my shopping bag, I found that most products were things I would not normally buy. For example, 4 cans of condensed milk. Now that I think about it, when I was in high school, the USSR was collapsing, and there were no good snacks or sweets. However, every house always had a can of condensed milk. It had a long shelf life. It was incredibly sweet, and it could be easily prepared. You can also put it on a bread and enjoy it. Even though I no longer eat it, to my own surprise, I bought it unconsciously at that time. Although I had hardly worried about having food at home before, I was then terribly worried about what I would do if I ran out of food. I remember cooking different dishes intensively every day for the first week of COVID-19 lockdown.

The other experience is my family memory. My father was a university dropout, and my grandfather lost his diploma because of World War II, as I previously mentioned in the part: "Where is My Home?" So everyone in my family supported education and felt that at least, just in case, we should have our academic documents in order and always with us.

After World War II, my grandmother, a young widow with children, remarried. Her husband Hryhoriy had also been married before. When he was drafted into the army, he had not brought his diploma and other documents with him. When he returned from the war, he found that his former wife had sold his diploma because she was having a tough time making ends meet. Unfortunately, the university archives were all burned down, and he could not get his certificate reissued because there was no proof of his education. After the war, he worked for a railway company and traveled around the country. When I was a child, I looked forward to hearing his stories from various places, but he would always say that he could have worked in Kyiv if he had something to prove his educational background.

Also, one of my research topics is the Ukrainian diaspora in Asia. Reading the documents of Ukrainians in China on the eve of WWII, one can see their struggle being there without proper documents and not being able to leave the country.

When I left for Vienna in early February of 2022, I put all my documents, including my university diploma and doctoral degree, in an organized file in my travel bag with trembling hands. It was two weeks before the Russian invasion. I did not know I would not be able to come back from a three-week trip as planned.

In fact, in early January, before the war broke out, I found out that the Chernihiv Historical Archive had documents that could trace my family history back to the 17th century. However, the Archive was badly damaged in an air raid in March. Seeing the shelled Archive, a museum, and houses on the news, I had to think about the attackers' motivation to erase the history of Ukraine as it is. I also was thinking how fragile Ukrainian history is. Also, the idea that those who are not on your side can make you vanish, to stop existing, erasing family history, is frightening.

Re-experiencing Trauma

Ukrainians have been through a lot of traumatic experiences. However, people have different thoughts on ways of dealing with trauma. There are those who do not care much about being traumatized, those who feel victimized and wonder why they have suffered such a painful experience, and those who slowly face their trauma and convert it to an opportunity for personal growth.

In the past 30 years since independence, the Ukrainian people have been living a normal life in their own country and worked hard to overcome the societal traumas of the past. Until recent days we did not have a custom to talk about our own feelings. Feelings were something that you keep to yourself and were better off not showing in public. I remember when I was crying at home as a child and teenager being overloaded with feelings, and my mom always told me to stop crying. Tears were something forbidden, something that will break you from within and something no one around you is able to cope with. Feelings somehow were considered a dangerous thing: a sign of weakness. Honestly, after being exposed to so much trauma in their families and in society, people simply did not have time and a space to digest and to accept them.

After the Chornobyl accident in 1986, people did not talk much about it at a family level, probably because they did not know what to do with that traumatic experience. However, if we look at the national level, the famine and other traumatic events are now properly included in history textbooks, while freedom of speech and expression is guaranteed and people can talk about them in the media and literature. Archives and museums have been built, and the fourth Saturday of November has become a Holodomor Memorial Day, a solemn day dedicated to remembering the victims of the Great Ukrainian Famine.

Just when we thought we were finally getting over our traumatic past, the Russian invasion has added other traumas. Those of the "war" itself, the trauma and guilt of seeking refuge in foreign countries, and many more. Many people were shocked to see tragic photos and videos of this war. You might call it "witness trauma," and it is not limited to Ukrainians. News about the war is reported internationally, therefore there are people around the world who are also in shock and cannot sleep.

Even if people fled to other countries and are staying away from the war, trauma may appear in their daily lives. For example, the trauma that lay dormant in the bodies of Ukrainians sent to Germany as cheap labor during World War II.

Two weeks after my friend's family evacuated to Hungary, the man who rented them a house asked her out of kindness if she would like to work in the greenhouse in the botanical garden nearby and have some small payment, and her elderly mother burst into tears. She said in tears: "Why do I have to pull weeds in the greenhouse at my age just to earn 5 euros per hour?" The person who suggested this had good intentions, thinking that taking care of the plants would heal her soul and 5 euros per hour was just a token payment. On the other hand, when that lady was a child, people around her were taken to Germany as cheap labor during the war. Crossing the border as a refugee she was afraid that she would be used in the same way with her very fragile status. They finally cleared up this matter and my friend's mother actually ended up never going to the green house. But was this just a misunderstanding or was it the effect of past societal traumas?

The Russian invasion has brought back many of these painful memories of the past. My mother is no exception. When she heard the air raid sirens, she recalled now when she was 5, she was hiding in a trench with other women and children at the beginning of World War II. It was dug by my grandmother in her garden. I had never heard this story before. To that trench, considered to be a shelter, my grandmother brought some food and served it with aluminum dishes and spoons on the shelves dug out of the ground. Then suddenly the air raid shelter was hit by an explosion, and the dishes fell to the ground and made a clattering sound. The sirens on February 2022 suddenly brought that memory to her mind. Hearing this story made me realize that human beings have many ways of remembering other than words, and that memories from long ago can suddenly resurface, brought to you by some unexpected, specific sound, for example.

The trauma-ridden minds of the Ukrainian people, which they had finally started to overcome, were once again damaged by the Russian invasion. It will take an unimaginably long time for them to recover. Ukraine, it seems, in the peaceful period after independence, did not have enough time and courage to discuss experiences during Soviet time, as well as reflect its relationship with Russia. Ukraine was busy keeping up with problems in the economy and other areas. I guess people are now regretting it. It would help to create proactive and healthier self-narratives for all of us. Now and after the war is over, it seems to me this it will be a significant issue to reconsider, not only at the national level but also at the family, as well as on the individual level too.

(September 1, 2022)

4. History of Migration

From Research to Reality: When My Study Became My Life

For the past eight years, I have delved into the fascinating history of Ukrainian migration across the Far East and Asia, focusing specifically on the interactive web of Ukrainian-Japanese collaborations in northeastern China during the tumultuous 1930s and 1940s.

While researching in Ukrainian, American and Japanese archives, I also focused on how Ukrainians lived and engaged in cultural activities in Asia from 1870 to 1945. In particular, during the three years of the COVID-19 outbreak, when I was reading in Kyiv the sources I had previously collected in the US, I felt as if the pain of those who had suffered so terribly as immigrants without identification papers was my own.

Before February 24th, I had never imagined in my wildest dreams that my research topic would become my own reality. I also went to the police in the evacuation area to apply for a new ID card and had my fingerprints taken. I was desperate to regain my identity and self-respect as a researcher. I was subjected to cruel criticism and other harsh treatment. I had to experience firsthand the historical facts that I had learned through my research.

In Shanghai in 1945, in order to receive a food coupon, an official had to check the home of the refugee. If they had cats at home, they would be considered rich and would not receive food coupons. In the spring of 2022, many Ukrainians evacuated with their dogs and cats, but it was difficult for them to find a place to live. Sometimes people assumed they were rich. I wondered about this historical coincidence. Many people in Ukraine say that they cannot abandon their animals because they are members of the family, but some have given them up due to this pressure.

If we have a look at the history, there have been 4 waves of emigration out of Ukraine. The purposes of people in these waves varied. The first wave was from the mid-1870s until World War I, when farmers and laborers from Western Ukraine went to Canada, the United States, and Brazil. As a result of the abolition of serfdom during this period, many people headed for the development of the Far East. Some moved to Australia, New Zealand, and Hawaii.

The second wave was between the First and Second World Wars and was mainly for social and political reasons. It might be said that those moved who did not want to live under the Soviet regime. Many went to Poland, Czechoslovakia, Romania, France, Germany, the US and Canada.

The third wave of immigrants began at the end of World War II and included ex-servicemen, those who were forced by the Nazis to come to Germany to do manual labor, those who became refugees due to the war and some other groups as well. Their destinations included the USA, Canada, Brazil, Argentina, and Australia. Some Ukrainian immigrants who were in Asia at that time moved to the US, South America, and Australia.

The fourth wave, which began with the collapse of the USSR, was due to economic reasons. The significant group was the immigrants from western Ukraine to the USA and Europe (Poland, Portugal, Italy, etc.), where women worked as helpers and babysitters and men as construction workers. Many migrant workers also went to Russia. Then there is the migration caused by the war in the eastern Ukraine in 2014 and the annexation of Crimea; many of those migrants moved to Poland and other countries, but this is not regarded as a separate wave of emigration.

However, many researchers have claimed that a fifth wave of emigration has been happening since the recent Russian invasion. Although the statistics are neither final nor certain as of yet, according to them, 12 million people have left the country since February 2022. It is not clear how many of these people will return if the war drags on. In any case, it is a tremendous number for a country of 43 million.

The Ukrainians who have fled their country have experienced all the same things as the immigrants before them. They often have few belongings, no proper identification, and are desperate to find a new home with their children and animals. It takes time to integrate into a new society due to the language barrier, so migrants often form communities with fellow Ukrainians. In the age of advanced social media, it is easy to connect and exchange information even in a new place. There are glee clubs, sock-knitting clubs, and volunteer groups that support evacuees and the army. Since most of the evacuees are women and children, there are many "women's clubs."

These people are living two lives. They mentally inhabit two countries: Ukraine and the one that has welcomed them. Even though they are physically abroad, a part of them remains in the homeland, staying connected by reading daily news, chatting with friends, accessing social media and paying monthly utility bills for their apartments back home. They hear from people about missile attacks every night and relatives and friends dying because of this war. It is all pretty intense compared to the experiences of previous generations of displaced people and migrants because social networks and internet news are constant, which sometimes makes it mentally challenging for those trying to stay focused on their work, studies and lives in their new places of residence.

Habits Developed from the Environment

Some people say that Ukrainian women do not look like refugees because they are well-dressed. When a Japanese friend of mine went to Italy for a business trip, a cab driver in Rome said to him: "Ukrainian women put a lot of effort into their clothes and beauty, so they don't look like the refugees we have seen so far." Even though the pandemic put them in their sportswear at home, they still put on makeup and paid attention to their clothes. During the Soviet era, people had few personal belongings, and wherever they went, they were often judged and treated differently based on their clothes. Hence, the custom of dressing up remains.

This reminded me of a story I heard from another Japanese acquaintance. I met a young CEO in Kyiv, who had his hair styled and dressed so well that he looked like a model in a men's magazine. He told me since he was not blessed with much money in his childhood, he had learned to be careful to avoid being called sloppy.

Past traumas can lead to different lifestyles. In one shelter in Europe, people were surprised to see a woman with a Louis Vuitton bag, even though she had almost no personal belongings.

When Ukrainians go out or even in the event of evacuation, they dress up neatly. It seems that some countries dress up and others dress down. When I went to Brazil in 2016, I first realized the opposite perspective prevailing in South America. If you look like you have money, you will be targeted, so they dress modestly on purpose.

Also, this war made people reveal some things they probably would never say to you before. I recently learned that the families of my two British friends I have known for more than 10 years were in fact refugees. One's father fled Egypt in the 1950s, and the other's grandfather was of Jewish descent and moved to the UK at the beginning of the 20th century. They had never talked about these things before, but the Russian invasion seems to have brought back their memories. They said: "At that time, a total stranger helped us. I wanted to return the favor, so I accepted a Ukrainian family." That Ukrainian my friend accepted was a complete stranger, but they did their best to find a job and rent their own house within a few months, which seems to improve the attitude towards Ukrainians in my friend's eyes. Thank goodness for that.

Nevertheless, many of them return to Ukraine because they cannot get used to living in a foreign country and someone else's house. A new language is difficult for them. Their social status has changed, leading to an identity crisis. Many women return to Ukraine because their fathers and husbands have not left and they want to live with their families. When deciding whether to continue living abroad or return to their homeland, Ukrainian mothers often listen to their children's opinions.

I have heard the following story from a child who was evacuated to Germany: "I want to go back to Kharkiv, but I am afraid of the attacks. I love my dad, but I do not want to leave my mom. I made friends at school in Germany. [When I said that] My mom and grandma chose to stay too." It's complicated, but I understand their situation. Whether these people will keep their identity, at least in terms of lifestyle and cultural activities, as former immigrants did, or integrate into the host society remains to be seen.

A neighbor of my friend's mother in her German apartment building put a message on the bulletin board that reads: "Frau K (Mrs. K) doesn't speak German, so please help her in her time of need." This inspired everyone to be kind. It seems that these small interactions between the refugees and the people who accept them will help them adjust to the new society.

I have met many different people in the past year. I once met refugees from Palestine. One family had been displaced for 7 years and another for 15 years. The daughter of the family that had been refugees for 7 years could speak many languages and was kind and willing to help people around them. The one who was a refugee for 15 years cried when she recalled her evacuation experience as a child, but was otherwise always cheerful. A friend who knew both families said: "The experiences of all the refugee families are equally harsh, but they probably think that they should not show their depressed feelings to others." I am not sure about that, but maybe it is true. At first, we try to help depressed people, but if it continues, the supporters may get tired of negative thinking and leave.

I do not know whether Ukrainians who have fled to other countries will be strong and cheerful or will have negative thoughts for a while due to the trauma from the war, but I hope that societies of countries they currently live in will accept them as they are.

(January 6, 2023)

5. Flag of Blue Sky and Wheat Field

During the Soviet Era, the Flag was Dangerous

There are few bicolored flags in the world which are divided horizontally into two parts with different colors. Only Poland, Monaco, Indonesia, and Ukraine have such flags. The Japanese flag, *Hinomaru*[19], also has two colors, but it is different.

In 1991, when Ukraine gained independence, the flag of a yellow wheat field and a blue sky became the national flag. It had been used even before that, but in the Soviet era, the mere possession of it was considered dangerous by the authorities. The yellow wheat field and the blue sky are a typical summer scene in the Ukrainian countryside, and the flag itself is a reminder of sentiments for the farmland that is wholeheartedly cared for. Still it was considered a symbol of "nationalists."

There is a statue of the national poet Taras Shevchenko in the park in front of the Kyiv National University, and every year on March 9th, his birthday, many people pay floral tribute to him. However, if they carried a yellow and blue flag, they were subject to a crackdown. In some cases, they could be sentenced to 2 years in prison.

One of my former teachers is from Lviv in the western part of the country. He was still a child when the Soviet army was stationed there in 1945 during the annexation of Western Ukraine, and he was severely beaten by Soviet soldiers when he put up the yellow and blue flags at his school. He said he still has the scars on his back.

In the year following independence in 1991, the student council of Kyiv National University made a university hoodie for the first time. It had a round framed picture of university on the chest, and the pattern came in distinct colors. There was a black and white logo, blue and white, and yellow and blue. Many students were told by their parents who saw them for the first

---

19   Means circle of the sun.

time that it is better not to wear the blue and yellow one outside. I suppose that the memories of the Soviet era were still too vivid for the parents of my generation, and they could not help but be concerned about the safety of their children. But many of us students came from home wearing ordinary sweaters and changed into hoodies in the restrooms of the university. After class, we would go to the restroom to change back into our sweaters and go home. Young people are indeed fearless.

For more than 20 years after independence, no one complained about having things of yellow and blue colors. After the war started in the East in 2014, pro-Russian people started accusing them of being "nationalists". The case of Stepan Chubenko, a boy who was a goalkeeper in a soccer club in Kramatorsk, Donetsk region in the east, who was beaten to death for wearing a yellow and blue ribbon on his backpack after his return from winter holidays in western Ukraine, was reported all over Ukraine. I too was shocked and devastated. I could not believe that such a tragedy could happen in these times.

Yet, after the Russian invasion in 2022, I have heard many such stories. There were many stories how people in the Russian occupied territories buried the flag in their yards.

On the other hand, since the beginning of the war, Ukrainian flags have often been spotted outside the country. Sometimes they were flown by refugees, and at other times by foreigners with a feeling of support for Ukraine. These two colors also became common in the fashion world. Yellow and blue have become a symbol not only of support for Ukraine, but also of freedom and independence. Some haute couture brands, such as Balenciaga (Spain) and Lever Couture, and many influencers such as the American fashion model Bella Hadid have started to use these colors in their collections. Furthermore, many people wore masks in Ukrainian colors to greet then Speaker of the US House of Representatives Nancy Pelosi when she visited Taiwan in August of 2022 during the COVID-19 pandemic. Less than a year after the invasion began, the colors came to represent not only freedom and independence, but also tenacity and fortitude. It is not an exaggeration to say these colors became the fashionable colors of the year 2022.

For the record, Sweden, Kazakhstan, Barbados in the Caribbean Sea, Bosnia and Herzegovina and Kosovo in the former Yugoslavia, and Palau in the Western Pacific also use yellow and blue on their flags, although in slightly different shades. Tokushima prefecture in Japan also has a prefectural flag using these two colors (yellow prefectural emblem on an indigo background, inspired by Tokushima's specialty indigo dyeing). The flag of the European Union also uses the same two colors. In the case of the Ukrainian flag, the blue means the blue sky, however, in other countries it is often used to represent water, rivers and the sea. The yellow color is most commonly attributed to wheat fields, but some believe it represents God.

How the Flag was Created

How did the Ukrainian flag become what it is today? Going back in history, the coat of arms of the city of Lviv in the 13th century had a yellow lion on a blue background, and the coat of arms of the "first Ukrainian state", the Principality of Galicia-Volhynia (1199-1349), which succeeded the Kyivan Rus, had the same two colors. The Cossacks, armed horsemen who settled on the steppes of Russia and Ukraine from around the 15th century, also used bicolor flags. In Ilya Repin's painting "Cossacks are Writing a Letter to the Turkish Sultan" painted in 1891, there is a soldier holding up a blue and yellow flag and a red and black flag wrapped around a pole. It is said that Repin consulted his friend, historian Dmytro Yavornytsky, for historical perspective and asked him to be the model for this painting.

Then, after the Russian Revolution, the Central Rada (Council) was established in Kyiv in March 1917, which governed Ukraine, and began to use the yellow and blue flag. In 1918, a competition was held to select the coat of arms of the Ukrainian state, and the painter Hryhorii Narbut submitted a proposal to use these two colors to represent the history of the Cossacks.

In fact, there was also a Ukrainian flag with a third color added during this period. The Ukrainians had settled in the Russian Far East from the Amur River to the Pacific coast, but when the Soviet side advanced into the region, the Ukrainians fled and tried to establish a state called "Green Ukraine." The flag of that state was yellow and blue, with the addition of green to represent the rich natural environment of the region.

However, Ukraine's independence and autonomy under the Central Rada was short-lived. After entering the Soviet Union and becoming the Ukrainian Soviet Socialist Republic, the flag changed to the red one with the letters "УРСР" [USSR] on it, and the yellow and blue flags were banned.

Even though it was banned in the Soviet Union, Ukrainian immigrants in the US and Canada often used that flag. On July 27th, 1976, in Montreal, Canada, during a soccer match between East Germany and the USSR, a young second-generation Ukrainian immigrant ran onto the field with a yellow and blue flag. He wanted to draw attention to the Soviet Union's suppression of Ukrainians' freedom. The flag was brought from abroad when the Ukrainian national soccer premier league resumed for the first time since the war started on August 23rd, 2022.

My own feeling for the flag has become stronger since the beginning of the war, and I think it is the same for all Ukrainians. The Ukrainian national soccer team used to hand out posters with the flag design to their supporters who came to watch their international games. The idea was that if everyone took them out from their seats and lined them up together, they would make a huge flag. The refugees were happy to receive them. I also heard that people who fled from the Russian occupied territories hid the Ukrainian flag in the lining of their suitcases.

Since the 2006 Winter Olympics in Torino, I have also been carrying the flag to cheer for my country each time I go to watch the Olympics. However, when I left Kyiv this time, I left that flag behind, not expecting I would need it. Nevertheless, after the invasion, I almost cried when I received it from my friend in Australia who bought the flag from Amazon. After all, I am certain that my feelings for the flag of my homeland have intensified since the war started.

(December 15, 2022)

III. Daily Life During Wartime

1. War Expressed in Art

Ukraine, the Land of Fine Arts

Ukraine has a tradition of producing many excellent works of art. There was a time when there was no freedom of expression, so people expressed their thoughts in art. It allowed people to communicate without speaking out. One prominent period of art was from the Russian Revolution to the 1930s. Many artists, including Mykhailo Boychuk (1882-1937), emerged. Ukrainian painters also participated in the Venice Biennale, an international exhibition of contemporary art, exhibiting 17 paintings in 1928 and 15 in 1930, significantly more than other Soviet republics. However, the oppression of Stalin in the 1930s prevented them from further participating in the exhibition.

I remember that a few years ago the National Art Museum of Ukraine in Kyiv held an exhibition of art of this period. Stalin not only ordered the painters be killed, but also planned to collect and destroy their works. Fortunately, there were people who hid and protected them. All the works were in good condition, but on some there was another painting on the back of the canvas. I was impressed by that. There were simply the boots of a soldier or a state security officer on the back of some paintings: the artist was lying on the floor, looking up at the officer. When I saw this, I felt the horror of those times.

When Russia annexed the Crimean Peninsula in 2014 and war broke out in eastern Ukraine, artists from the east immediately began to express these events in their art. The work of Zhanna Kadyrova, exhibited at the Pinchuk Museum of Contemporary Art in Kyiv in the fall of 2014, was very impressive. There was a map of Ukraine made of bricks and "Crimea" bricks were crumbled on the floor. I was reminded once again of the power of art.

Since the Revolution of Dignity in 2014, graffiti and murals have increased in the streets of Kyiv. The portraits of Taras Shevchenko, a national poet of the mid-19th century, Ivan Franko, a poet active in the 20th century, and Lesya Ukrainka, another poet, on the building of the Academy of Sciences near Hrushevsky Square, the battlefield, were incredibly impressive. All of them dedicated their lives to national liberation and movements for cultural development. They were represented as present-day fighters, wearing bandanas and military masks. Shevchenko's mural was accompanied by the words "The fire does not burn the hardened!" The one of Franko has the words "Our whole life is a war," and the one of Lesya Ukrainka reads "He who has set himself free will always be free." I felt that the ban on Ukrainian language and culture in the Russian Empire during the 19th century is still relevant for present-day Ukrainians and is deeply connected to the spirit of the Revolution of Dignity.

The number of murals has increased greatly in the last 8 years. For example, one on Velyka Vasylkivska Street, 111/113 depicting students who were killed at the fight of Kruty village during winter of 1918, also others around the city there are many historical figures, such as Mykhailo Hrushevsky, historian and the first president of Ukraine in 1918, Pavlo Skoropadsky, the last Hetman, and Symon Petliura, Supreme Commander of the Ukrainian People's Army of that period, as well as Lesya Ukrainka.

The number of murals with themes of Ukrainian culture and folktales has also increased. For instance, there is a work titled "Resurrection" on the Andriivskyi Descent, a collaboration between a Ukrainian and a French artist. A young girl in traditional costume with a garland of flowers on her head is gorgeous and impressive. The artist says that when the colors fade due to weathering, she paints over again. On the other hand, some conservative people in Ukraine are critical of murals, saying that they cover up the old parts of buildings without repairing them properly. However, looking at St. Sofia cathedral in Kyiv, we can assume that since citizens of Kyiv have been painting graffiti for 1000 years, it can be assumed that this art has previously existed in Kyiv, evolved over time, and now spread to cover the entire walls of buildings. Recently, the number of murals has dramatically increased, and they have become a landmark of the city, gradually changing the face of Kyiv.

Art as a Form of Resistance

Even before February 24th, Ukrainian illustrators began to create posters that made the viewer feel alarmed. I still remember well the one that showed a bouquet of tulips decorated with ribbons and a hand grenade hanging from it, saying "We do not greet the occupiers with flowers."

For a while after the start of Russian aggression, the artists were at a loss what to do, devastated like the rest of the citizens. They thought what was happening could not be real. However, after some time, various works of art began to appear. In early March 2022, the British newspaper *The Guardian* published an illustration by Sergiy Maidukov[20], who was known abroad even before the war. That illustration was war-related and, as in his previous works, the use of colors is very impressive. Oleksandr Grekhov[21] portrays the poet Shevchenko as a soldier in a modern style. His illustrations are brightly colored and have a unique sense of humor. His art works are available for sale on Instagram, and the author is sending a part of profit for donations to the army. In addition, there is "Cat called Fig," a smart and mischievous cat created by painter Olena Pavlova, who encourages the people of Ukraine[22].

Many of the new murals are war related. In May 2022, Saint Javelina (Saint Mary Magdalene holding a Javelin, an American-made man-portable anti-tank system) was created at Antonovycha Str., 13, however the halo was removed because of complaints from church officials. There also is a mural of Patron the dog, who works for the State Emergency Service of Ukraine in Chernihiv and became famous for finding bombs during the war. In the summer, a mural of a mythical air force pilot with the nickname "The Ghost of Kyiv"[23] was created. And in November, a British street artist called Banksy painted "Kids Playing" which depicts

---

20 Instagram: sergiymaidukov
21 Instagram: unicornandwine
22 Instagram: kit_inzhyr
23 "The Ghost of Kyiv" is a composite character representing the actions of the entire Ukrainian air force.

two children using a metal tank trap as a seesaw spray-painted onto a concrete defensive block at the Independence Square in Kyiv. In Irpin, they painted a female gymnast balancing on a pile of rubble.

Similar to the famous artists, citizens were silent for the first few weeks with the question haunting them: "Why? For what reason were we attacked?" After they regained composure, more people started to write their diaries, even if they were just scribbles. I am one of them. These diaries and drawings have a particularly important meaning, as even after the war is over, the records will remain, and they will be the proof that people managed to survive even in the darkest of times.

From October 2022, missile attacks increased, and power outages occurred repeatedly in Ukraine. Around that time, my acquaintance's child Zhenya asked her parents to buy her white pencils and black paper for drawing. When the parents asked her why, she replied that it was the best way to express the current situation. Zhenya, a girl from Kharkiv, was 8 years old when she was evacuated from the city to the village in Kharkiv region, where she had been living for more than half a year. As a city girl who had never lived in the village before, she had been exposed to many animals and plants and had been painting them for a while. However, when the power went out, her painting style changed in an instant. The scenery was the same, but the colors disappeared from the pictures along with the electricity, and they became black and white. This was her way of expression.

My friend Valentyn, who is a photographer, has been taking pictures of famous Ukrainian artists for almost 10 years. After the war started, he started to take pictures of evacuees in the evacuation centers. If you look at the faces of the people you can see the hardships of the war. His photo is also on the cover of this book. It is depicting his one-year-old son, who was born just before the war. In Ukraine we have expression for the older generation of people who were born before and during WWII. We call them "children of war". My mother is one of them. Unfortunately, from now on we will use the same expression for all children growing up during this war.

After the war began, many people moved to western Ukraine. However, the drama theater in Ivano-Frankivsk did not stop working even for a day. On the contrary, the actors worked twice as hard as before. During the day they collected relief supplies and distributed them to the evacuees, and at night they worked as usual in the theater. There were two queues at the theater every day. In the afternoon people stood to receive relief supplies and, in the evening, to watch the play. There was a missile attack in the middle of the performance, so the performance was moved to the basement and continued even during the air raid. The theater was used as a shelter throughout the war, and many people took shelter in that basement during the performances. It is reported that as many as 500 people were sheltered from February to April of 2022. It has been a year since the war, and the theater has introduced a new play. The modern adaptation of the verse drama "The Forest Song" written by the abovementioned poet Lesya Ukrainka has been especially well received.

The number of Ukrainian art exhibitions outside of the country has also increased during the past year. One of the most impressive exhibition called "In the Eye of Storm. Modernism in Ukraine 1900-1930" was held in January 2023 in Madrid, Spain, which presented Ukrainian art of the modernist period from the 1900s to the 1930s[24]. Visitors could see the continuity of artistic tradition, the connection to modern art and society of Ukraine, and the usage of vivid colors in the past as well. It was sad to think about the fate of many Ukrainian artists who were killed by Stalin's regime. I wonder how many great works of art they would have left behind if they had lived.

In the past year, there were museums shelled and destroyed in Ukraine — the museum of Maria Prymachenko, famous for her childlike, naïve art, the house-museum of self-taught artist Polina Raiko (in Oleshky, Kherson Region, which was flooded by a dam

---

24 The same exhibition called "In the Eye of Storm. Modernism in Ukraine 1900-1930" was held in Royal Academy of Arts in London between June-October 2004.

breach), the museum of the philosopher Hryhorii Skovoroda in Kharkiv region, and The Bohdan and Varvara Khanenko National Museum of Arts in Kyiv, which was damaged by the October 2022 missile attack—it seems that Russia has envy for the free and rich expression of Ukrainians, and there is a strange continuity back to the oppressive period of the 1930s.

(January 26, 2023)

2. Laughing at War

The Importance of Laughter in the Midst of War

When a representative of an international financial institution, which funds my friend's company, visited Ukraine for the first time in a year after the war started, his face was constantly sad. He seemed to think that war is a sorrowful thing and therefore he should not smile. However, he was incredibly surprised when my friend told him: "Our employees are still laughing and joking with each other at work, and that is the strength of life."

It is true that it may seem incredible for foreigners. However, Ukrainians have tenacity, and perhaps, anger and laughter help them to keep their spirits up.

Stand-up comedy (improvised storytelling) has also become extremely popular in the past year. Previously there had predominantly been comedians from Russia performing in Russian in this genre. However, since the beginning of the invasion, a number of Ukrainian performers have come out, performing in Ukrainian. Some of them are women.

One of them, Anya Kochehura, is particularly interesting[25]. The themes of her talk ranged from everyday life after February 24th to politics, and although sometimes the topics are dark, they could make people laugh.

I would like to retell some of her jokes.

- A friend of mine called to tell me that she went to a quest call "Room of Fear" over the weekend. I wonder if fear is in short supply now that the war is in its seventh month. If I were you, I would go to "Room of Tranquility." A room with a rainbow and no enemies. But there is no such room.
- Since the invasion, curfews have been imposed in many residences, but not in our apartment building. We have been living with a curfew for a long time because of the

---

25   https://www.youtube.com/watch?v=7aGf2bL9AIQ

rules imposed by our concierge, an elderly woman. Even before war had started.
- The first to return to Kyiv among those who had evacuated to various places were those who had taken refuge with relatives. On February 26th, they came back after a fight.
- I did not think the war would be like this. There are deaths, tragedies, horrors, AND shisha restaurants are still open. Why do we deserve it? One can run from the missiles, holding a matcha latte in one hand. It is easier now to die in Kyiv from an accident with an electric scooter than from a missile attack. People are riding on those scooters in groups of three, we have to do something!
- Since February 24th, I have discovered a new meaning to social networks. 10 years ago I would not believe that I, as an ordinary person, can write in Twitter to the German Chancellor Scholz. I have discovered the power of Twitter and spend about 20 hours a day on it. It is unbelievable that I, as an ordinary person, can say "asshole" to a great German politician. I can easily talk to complete strangers. I can simply say: "German Chancellor Scholz is useless," and they immediately respond, and the conversation can last for 2 hours. When I run out of things to say, I just add, "President Macron is useless too," and the conversation continues.
- I was disappointed in the international organizations, as they were not what we thought they were. UN, NATO, Amnesty International, etc. I have some questions for the EU. Hungary is among its members. Is it only me who has an impression they did not really check that they were in compliance with the requirements to become a member? It does not seem like a well-thought out decision. [Looks at shoe] Cannot remove Orban. Then they came to us with a pile of papers. Was that written in font size 72? And were the questions like "What is your favorite color?" Also the service there is not good. One of my followers is living in Germany and she wrote that she had deposited cash at an

ATM on Thursday evening and would receive money on her card only the next Tuesday. I replied "Are the banknotes going to the bank by themselves on foot? Or is it Scholz who is personally counting every one? Is that why he is so busy?"
- If you are a talking behind the back of your friend, you are a bad person, yet if you gossip about the German Chancellor or the French President, you are honored to be called a responsible citizen, aware of current affairs.

Her storytelling has gained popularity because she is targeting ambiguous political rhetoric. It can be said that she expresses what people want to say but are not allowed to.

Everyone laughs when listening to her stories, but there is a lot of black humor. It is common that humor becomes darker in wartime. However, the few female comedians have never talked about politics before, and it is worth noting that young people's interest in politics has been growing. It also shows the fortitude of Ukrainians who are trying their best to overcome the reality of war with laughter, even though it hurts.

(April 17, 2023)

3. On Everyday Life

Power Outage as a Part of Daily Life

Since the beginning of the war, everyday life has gone wrong. As I wrote in the section "The War and Smartphones", I check the news on my smartphone right after I wake up in the morning. Sometimes I check the news more than 30 times a day, and before going to bed too. I ask my friends, relatives, and students for the news around them. After a certain period of time, I realized that I would go crazy if I kept doing this, so I became more cautious. But I still kept checking the news over and over again.

Around last May, I was talking to a famous Ukrainian football player who apparently was doing the same thing as me. He said that he checks the news before he goes to practice, during breaks, and after practice. He told me that he has a fear of missing out and has become more nervous than before.

After that conversation, spring ended, summer passed, and autumn came. Before autumn, the situation in Kyiv had slightly stabilized, and everyone was getting somewhat accustomed to the new situation and returning to normal life. Quite a few children returned from abroad. Then on October 7th, there was another attack and missiles hit the ground in front of Kyiv National University. I was shocked when I received photos of buildings that were next to the university—the publishing house that published my two books and the Khanenko family home now called Khanenko Fine Arts Museum, who made their fortune in the production and sale of sugar—the blast blew out the windows. I was shocked especially because I knew the place well.

I called a friend in Kyiv and asked her if she was was she alright. All I got was "As usual." She has never been a talker, but in her current condition, I guess "as usual" meant "fine". I have also heard a story about a young mother walking with her baby in a stroller in the corridor on the 18th floor of the apartment building. When someone asked her why she did not go outside, she replied that the elevator was not working due to the power outage and it was extremely difficult to go downstairs and back up. So, she decided to walk with her baby inside.

Recently my Japanese friends often ask me: "What is the daily life of a Ukrainian like?" Even though the power is out and water is not pumped to the apartments, people still have to pay their utility bills. If burglars find out that you have evacuated and have been away from home for a while and your flat is not protected by a police security system, you may be robbed, so people ask a friend or neighbor to check on their place from time to time. One of my university friends told me he is holding ten keys from his friends' and relatives' apartments in Kyiv.

Since the electricity is cut off, there are only a few places where you can pay for your groceries with a credit card. You need cash. However, you may not be able to withdraw money from ATMs because of the power outage. You have to do laundry and cook when there is still power on.

Additionally, many people have been experiencing sleepless nights due to the ongoing missile attacks, leading to prolonged sleep deprivation. A friend of mine shared a story about how he used to take melatonin to help him fall asleep. He stopped because during a night-time attack, the melatonin made it difficult for him to react quickly and hurry to the shelter.

There are people who continue living in buildings hit by missiles that are beyond repair. They have nowhere else to live and are afraid to go outside the country as they have no friends there. It is complicated in many ways. However, people tend to adjust even to the most complicated situations.

Different Daily Routines

When I asked people how they felt when the war started, many of them replied that at first they were stunned by disbelief, then filled with anger, and now they are getting used to it.

One of my former students Lida who went to Poland in December for the first time since the war started said: "When I saw the lights in Warsaw, my first thought was about energy consumption. Even though there are no power outages in Poland, somehow I could not believe it, so I charged my phone and powerbanks every night before going to bed. I was very nervous." She was angry that in Ukraine people are dying every day, but in Poland no one cares about it and people are living their normal lives. She was also a little jealous. Sometimes she cried because she felt sorry for herself. She eventually returned to live a normal life in Ukraine with her family. She said: "I will continue to pay taxes in Ukraine and wait for our victory." I did not know what to reply.

Another former student Tanya, who had taken refuge in the UK, came back to her home in the western city of Ternopil for a week at the beginning of the year. She later told me that the power went out for more than 6 hours every day and that she could not use the elevator or refrigerator. She laughed that she had to go up and down the stairs to the 9th floor several times a day to exercise her back. And even if you cook a meal, you cannot store it, so you have to eat it before the end of the day. She said that it was as if she had returned to the lifestyle of a few decades ago and that it was very difficult.

Maria, another student, who went abroad for the first time in December, came back to Kyiv because she could not get used to the stable life without power outages. She jokingly said: "I am so used to the situation in Kyiv that I may not be able to live under normal circumstances from now on. I did not have much in common with my old friends who I used to be close to. When I talked about the war, they immediately switched to other topics, which made me feel uncomfortable. I know I am traumatized, but I cannot help it."

I guess that is true. Different people receive information and process trauma in different ways. Even if you think it has no effect on you, your body still subconsciously reacts to a lot of information. Some people wake up at 3 a.m. because they are scared, some take sleeping pills but still cannot sleep, some take antidepressants. It is not easy to evacuate to another country. Some people have to work hard in a new environment, but they cannot do anything but watch the news of war everyday. There are people who cannot explain their medical condition to local doctors when they get sick.

Many of them are too old to learn the language and cannot go anywhere by themselves. One such person was Grandpa Sasha, who lived in city of Dnipro in the central part of the country and was brought to Germany by a volunteer group after his house was destroyed. He spoke beautiful Ukrainian and was very cheerful, but as soon as he was asked about his family, he answered with a sad look in his eyes: "I am all alone in the world." Alone... Yet in this war, many people feel left alone.

Trying to Protect the Usual Lifestyle

Lately, I cry easily at the slightest thing. Sometimes I cry after reading the news or talking with friends. The other day, I cried when I was told at the immigration checkpoint at the border in Germany: "A Ukrainian passport is good nowadays. You can go anywhere you want now." All I could reply was: "Thank you, but I don't think it is good when your home is taken away and my country is being destroyed... I want peace to return to Ukraine." The other person looked startled.

In Kyiv delivery workers are working as usual under the sky with flying missiles. Nowadays you can order medicine, clothes, food online. Before the war, this would be something trivial, but under these circumstances, everyone is grateful for it.

My close friend who is CEO of a company with 600 employees in western Ukraine told me that she holds her meetings in a shelter. When I asked her if it was because there was an air raid alarm, she said that there was no air raid that day, but she decided to work in the shelter because it was too much trouble to change the place every time there was an alarm, and she was tired of going up and down to the shelter. Everyone is tired, but still trying to protect their normal life.

Her husband, who is a foreigner, and their primary school aged daughter have taken refuge in the country of her husband's parents. She is living alone and using her training gym at home as a shelter. On New Year's Day this year, her family got together at their home in Lviv and went to the theater to see "The Nutcracker," dressing up for the occasion. However, an air raid alarm sounded at the bell, and they had to evacuate to the theater basement. It took an hour and a half for the alarm to be lifted, so the performance was eventually canceled. They sent me a photo. It was painful to see them all dressed up and sitting in a shelter.

Also, internet is not always working. There was no signal in Kyiv because of the power outage, and many of my friends could not be reached by phone. But when there is electricity, people tend to enjoy their lives even more. The other day, I tried to call my friend, but I could not get through at first. When I finally got through, she said: "I am sorry, I cannot talk to you at the moment, I am going to the cinema. For a date." The everyday life in wartime is sometimes unimaginable to those who are not in Ukraine: a date at the cinema after the electricity is back and the air raid alarm has been lifted.

In the meantime, the number of people getting married is increasing in Ukraine. In the first half of 2022, the number increased by 20 percent compared to the same period of the previous year. Daily life in Ukraine is conducted as usual, with funerals for many of the deceased, birthday parties with relatives, weddings, and so on. Ukrainians are trying to live to the fullest despite the difficult situation.

(February 6, 2023)

4. Ukraine and Japan

The First Day of a Series of Online Lectures

The year 2022 was the 30th anniversary of the establishment of diplomatic relations between Ukraine and Japan. As the pandemic was still ongoing, the university where I teach was going to hold a series of online lectures by prominent Japanese professors and former prominent diplomats. We held an opening ceremony and on the morning of the first lecture, the Russian invasion began. I called in panic to one of the professors who had been asked to give the lecture and canceled it. When I told him that I was praying for a quick end to the war, this former diplomat replied to me: "This war may go on for a long time" and I was left shocked and speechless. A year has passed since then, but the war is still going on. Unfortunately, the lecture series has been postponed.

The reason for organizing the lecture series was that Ukrainians still do not have many opportunities to visit Japan and have few chances to get in touch with Japanese. In the past, a Google search for Japan and Japanese in Ukrainian language brought only results such as "beautiful Japan", "tourist attractions", "differences between Japanese and Chinese", and that was all. Since independence, the number of Ukrainians studying abroad and traveling has increased. However, information about Japan is limited and even fewer people have contact with ordinary Japanese people. Having studied in Japan for master's and doctoral degrees, I know many researchers and I wanted to provide some valuable knowledge to the students through a series of lectures.

I first came to Japan to study in the spring of 1994. It was my first experience abroad. My friend said, laughing yet worrying: "You should go to Poland first, then Germany, then the USA, and only then Japan. If you go to Japan first, it will be too much of a shock. It's too different". However, even having seen many Japanese prints and sumi-e paintings and read translated works of Japanese literature since I was a child, I still had much to learn. Therefore, I wanted to bring back to Ukraine what I learned in Japan about language, history, ideology, culture, and international politics.

Japan Becoming Well Known in Ukraine

When I returned to Kyiv in the summer of 1994, I brought back a lot of things I had eaten in Japan, thinking that perhaps I could make them in Ukraine. Among them were a set for making sushi rolls and some instant noodles. When I invited my friends to a party, they were amazed at the food. It was so different from the meat- and potato-based meals we usually had. Almost 30 years have passed since then. Various Japanese foods have been introduced to Ukraine. In the beginning of the 2000s, there were many sushi restaurants opening in Kyiv. There were also fast food restaurants open 24 hours a day, which were popular among students. Ramen noodles have also become popular in the past few years, and I often saw many office workers going to eat ramen for lunch. And now, matcha lattes are served in trendy coffee shops. No one is exclaiming like in the old days: "A tea made from powder? Unbelievable!" They drink it as if it's something normal.

There are only two Japanese restaurants run by Japanese people in Kyiv, while all others are run by local people. The affection of Ukrainians toward Japanese cuisine arrived in Kyiv before the Japanese. Japanese chefs and managers had not yet taken advantage of the Japanese food boom. Once the news reached Japan, and it was about time for Japanese people to open restaurants in Ukraine, the Russian invasion started, which made things even more difficult.

There is a long history of Ukrainian people's love for Japan. Since the Soviet era, Ukrainians loved Japanese culture, and many literary works were translated into Ukrainian from the 1970s. Movies by Akira Kurosawa, music by Ryuichi Sakamoto and Kitaro, TVs and Walkmans by Sony were popular. People thought of Japan as of the land of robots. It could be said that they were carried away by the Orientalism of the Soviet Union.

It is the generation of people in their mid-40s and above who have this image. The younger generation was raised on Japanese pop culture. Starting with Tamagotchi and Furby, many young people became interested in Japan and the Japanese language through manga, anime, Pokemon, and other forms of Japanese culture.

The places where you can study Japanese language have multiplied. Only in Kyiv can you study Japanese as a major or optional subject at more than 10 universities. Most of the young people who enter the Japanese language department are interested in anime and manga, but since learning Japanese is difficult, many of them change their major if they are not lucky enough to study abroad by their third academic year.

However, they face the reality that there are almost no job opportunities after graduation. Although trading companies and the embassy hire people who can speak Japanese, they cannot advance in their careers. In this day and age, it is impossible to become anything other than a linguist if you can speak the language, and considering the days invested in studying, it is a waste of time and money. However, many students who study Japanese have excellent grades, so even if they give up Japanese, they can study international relations, economics, or marketing in the USA or Europe, start a business, or join a foreign company, and become quite successful. But it takes courage. Not all young Ukrainians who have strong ties with their parents and families are able to do so. At least it was like that until this war began.

Those who studied in Japan have courage. There are successful people who have started their own companies and connect Ukraine and Japan through trade.

In the last 10 years, the relations with Japan have intensified not only in politics, but also in culture, sports, etc. In the fall of 2012, on the occasion of the 20th anniversary of diplomatic relations, with the support of the Japan Foundation, Japanese Noh performers and Urasenke tea masters visited Kyiv, Lviv, and Donetsk, and a big festival was held. Since then, every autumn the Embassy holds a Japanese Film Festival, where many of Hayao Miyazaki's movies are shown.

Moreover, some words of Japanese origin have also been added to the Ukrainian vocabulary. Until now it was only *geisha*, *rickshaw, kimono,* but now it includes *manga, anime, sushi,* and ramen. These days, Ukrainians are becoming interested in Marie Kondo's decluttering *"Konmari", Kintsugi*—Japanese porcelain restoration, *Kaizen* as an improvement for business processes, and so on.

Thanks to Twitter, Ukraine and Japan were getting closer even in the midst of the COVID-19 outbreak. In January 2021, I caught a cold and was bored, so I started tweeting in a light mood. When I wrote about the Ukrainian custom of making bread birds in spring, I was surprised to see 7000 followers of my account at once. I felt the great power of social networking. I longed to be able to speak directly to a wider audience, but one should be cautious with it, as it also can become addictive.

After the War Broke Out

After the annexation of Crimea, the Japanese Prime Minister Shinzo Abe visited Ukraine for the first time and provided extensive economic support. Since the beginning of the Russian invasion, Ukraine has received a lot of political support and economic assistance from Japan, which made us feel closer. We share the same complicated feelings toward our common neighbor Russia. Japan, which until now had little information about Ukraine, has gained further understanding after the invasion. President Volodymyr Zelenskyy was the first Head of state in the history of Japan, among all world leaders, to address the National Diet of Japan online. Even on TV, Ukraine has been mentioned in variety shows, lunchtime programs, and so on, which was unthinkable in the past. The number of times the topic of Ukraine was brought up is astoundingly high. There used to be only a few programs about Ukraine every year, but now a major TV channel is receiving more than 200 applications from producers for making programs on Ukraine every quarter. Of course, not all of them are making it to the TV screen, but interest and supply are high.

It may sound like a joke, but in the mid-1990s, when I first came to Japan I was asked "Where are you from?" and I said "Ukraine", I was then asked either "Soviet Union or Russia?" or

"Did you mean Uruguay?" After the Orange Revolution of 2004, I was then asked "Western or eastern Ukraine?" After the Revolution of Dignity of 2014, when I said "Ukraine," people asked "Kyiv, Crimea, or Donetsk?" After February 2022, more specific place names became known, such as "Bucha, Irpin in Kyiv region, or Dnipro, or Kharkiv?" People's knowledge of Ukrainian geographical names has increased dramatically. It is much appreciated amidst all the misfortune. I wish that people had come to know about Ukraine in a different way. I wanted them to know Ukraine for its long history and culture of more than a thousand years, beautiful songs, rich nature, delicious food, kind and hospitable people, and so on.

The response of the Japanese government to the Russian invasion to Ukraine was swift. As the only non-Western member of the G7, Japan strongly supported Ukraine. According to the website of the Prime Minister's Office in April 2022, shortly after the invasion, 6 meetings on Ukraine were held, including two press conferences by the Prime Minister of Japan. This was a record in the history of 30 years of diplomatic relations. Japan's support for Ukraine started with the Revolution of Dignity and became stronger after the occupation of Crimea. In June 2015, then Prime Minister Shinzo Abe visited Ukraine for the first time. I was given the honor of guiding him around the St. Sophia Cathedral, that has history of over one thousand years.

Since the Prime Minister arrived late, I had the chance to talk with his spouse Mrs. Akie while I was waiting. I got a strong impression of her, and she surprised me by complimenting my shoes.

Then Prime Minister Abe listened carefully to the history of Ukraine and told us that Todaiji Temple in Nara, although it is a wooden structure, was built a little earlier than the St. Sophia Cathedral. Once the tour finished, he asked to return to the altar of St. Sophia Cathedral and meditate in silence. When I heard the news of Prime Minister Abe's death, the image of him in front of the altar of St. Sophia Cathedral came to my mind.

After the start of Russian aggression, Japanese aid amounted to 600 million euros, and for the first time in history, there was non-military aid from the Self-Defense Forces. Japan has slightly relaxed their strictest visa standards in the world to accept more than two thousand Ukrainian refugees. Not only Kyoto, the sister city of Kyiv, accepted Ukrainians, but all the prefectures in Japan. Many universities have created special courses for Ukrainian university students and some of them even offered courses in Ukrainian language. The cultural exchange that Ukrainian diplomats have been working so hard to promote for more than 30 years has accelerated. I wish it would have developed in this manner without the war though.

NHK, a major Japanese broadcaster, has a Ukrainian version of its website, and continues to provide useful information for refugees, as well as foreign and domestic news in Ukrainian, which is especially useful for understanding Japanese culture and Japanese people.

Furthermore, Japan has finally understood that Ukraine is not Russia, nor does it have the same culture as Russia, as they had thought before. Lev Mechnykov (Lev Mechnikov), who introduced anarchism to Japan, his brother Ilya Mechnykov (Elie Metchnikoff), a Nobel Prize-winning biologist, Vasyl Eroshenko (Vasili Eroshenko), a blind man supported by the restaurant named Nakamuraya in Shinjuku, General Roman Kondratenko, who tried to defend the fortified position of Port Arthur, and Lieutenant-General Kuzma Derevyanko, the representative of the Soviet Union at the ceremonial signing of the written agreement on the battleship Missouri that established the armistice ending World War II—were all Ukrainians. Not Russians, as it was considered before in Japan.

The exchange between Japan and Ukraine might have first started in the Russian Far East and Siberia back in the 19th century. Ukrainian peasants, freed from serfdom and dissatisfied with the land they received, took advantage of the Russian imperial government's promotion of development projects in the Far East and moved far away. The numbers may vary according to different statistics, but approximately one million Ukrainians migrated to the Far East between 1875 and 1917. Following the Russian Revolution, migrants began to emphasize their ethnic rights and tried to establish an autonomous political entity called "Green Ukraine." Ukrainian language newspapers and schools were established, and 4 of All-Ukrainian Far Eastern Congress were held between 1917 and 1918. Migrants also drafted the constitution of "Green Ukraine."

The Ukrainians were serious about their independence and wanted Japan, which was in the process of sending troops to Siberia to join the foreign intervention at that time, to assist them. The Ministry of Foreign Affairs of Japan also noticed the considerable number of Ukrainians in the Far East at the beginning of the 20th century and issued several reports on it. The Japanese also cooperated with the Ukrainian community in Manchuria in 1930s and let them publish newspapers in Ukrainian. Having Russia as a neighbor, the countries had mutual concerns. One can imagine what went through minds of Japanese people when they saw the fierceness of the Russian invasion.

Such a rapid deepening of relations and mutual understanding between both countries is a little blessing in these trying times. I hope that we can overcome this challenging moment and stay in touch with each other in peaceful times.

(March 9, 2023)

IV. Losses and Gains

1. War and Friendship

My Students, My Friends Abroad

In the 10 years I have been teaching in the Department of History at the National University of Kyiv Mohyla Academy, I have had contact with about 900 students in total through lectures and seminars on Japanese and Ukrainian history. I have stayed in contact with students even after their graduation, and many of them have come to me for advice.

When Russia invaded on February 24th, five of my students asked: "Dear professor, are you all right? Let me know if there is anything I can do to help you." Of the five, two women were in the UK and Poland, and the remaining three men stayed in Ukraine. One of the three men has left his studies abroad and returned to Ukraine to start a volunteer organization. Another one has joined the army, and the third one is helping the local territorial defense forces. One of them lives in the west of Ukraine and sheltered my family for a while. I still frequently contact these five people. While everyone was so desperate to protect themselves that they did not have time to think about others, my friends outside the country reacted quickly. They asked me if I was safe, and before I could write "I am alright", they asked me: "Please, tell me your account number. You will surely need money so I will transfer some to your account." I was very moved because some of them had tough times in their own lives. I thanked them for their worry but refused to accept their kindness.

People who Turned out not to be Friends

However, as I am a researcher, the thing that was much more important to me than my safety and money was to preserve my academic path even under such circumstances. I looked for a job at a Japanese university, and many people assisted me in that search. I would like to express my gratitude again to all of them who helped me. However, there were also times when people

I considered friends turned out not to be. This was not only my experience, but also a problem that may occur in the future, so I shall write about it. There were several unfortunate cases.

First, there were cases of certain bureaucratic callousness, if you can call it that, under the guise of fairness. For example, I once received the following response: "Supporting Ukrainian researchers is a critical issue, but the situation is so diverse and dynamic that neither academic societies nor universities have yet agreed on a coherent policy. I understand that you are having a hard time, however there are potentially many researchers who need more support, such as those who lived in areas that were occupied by Russia or those whose homes were destroyed by the war, and frankly speaking, it seems to me that it would be quite difficult to invite people who have already evacuated to a foreign country and are safe for the time being, to our university for a long period of time when we have not had any particular interaction with them before."

Those of us who have escaped the war can only think of how peaceful our surroundings are. Incidentally, this university has not accepted a single Ukrainian researcher to date.

Secondly, there were cases of being lectured on how to live. When I said that I was looking for a teaching or research position, I was advised that "in such situation as yours, you should leave behind the academic path and throw away your degrees and look for a normal job." That person was a businessperson, so he might sincerely give this "advice". However, I wondered how he, who had studied abroad, thought about the global mobility of human resources. Another acquaintance said to me upfront: "Since you are a displaced person, you should know your place and put aside this strange pride—trying to be an academic."

Thirdly, there were cases when people demanded repayment of favors. There is a useful expression *Ue kara no mesen wo* in Japanese meaning "patronizing." Some people who, when I expressed my gratitude for providing me a place to stay for a few weeks and told them that I had been fortunate to find a research position and wanted to leave, reprimanded me: "Do you understand that we allowed you to stay here merely out of goodwill? We did so because we wanted you to work hard here in the future."

Finally, there were cases of people who were insensitive to other people's misfortune or, worse, tried to benefit from it. Currently, the word "Ukraine" attracts a lot of attention. These people were continuously saying "I will give you my support," however, upon a closer look, I could not help but wonder if they were just trying to look good in the public eye.

A researcher I once met has been continuously liking my Twitter posts for 6 months since the Russian invasion. I was grateful for that, but I wondered why he did not send me an email directly asking me if I was okay, even though he knew my email address. When I asked him about it, he replied: "I was not sure how to ask you about the current situation." He is a very shy person; however, he keeps appearing on Japanese TV and newspapers, saying that he is very worried about the situation in Ukraine, yet he avoided asking people directly involved about the actual situation. He repeatedly pushes a like button to the posts to show that he cares. However, when it comes to approaching those in need, he is shy.

Moreover, there was the following case. Someone said, "I can help you to find work in the field of cooperation between Japan and Ukraine," but the more I listened, the clearer it became that their main purpose was to look good in the public eye, namely, in front of the relevant authorities, by taking care of Ukrainian refugees. When I thanked him for his kindness and politely declined the offer, he began approaching places saying, "She is doing fine. There is no need to help her." Later, when I consulted with a certain organization about employment, that person had "advised" them not to hire me. He has attended many events wearing a blue and yellow tie symbolizing support for Ukraine, but his interior views are unclear.

I hoped the above is only my personal experience, but my friends who are in the same position have been in similar situations. Compared to Western countries, Japan may not be accustomed to refugees and displaced persons, but as much as I like Japan and its people, I hope that will change in the future.

What is a True Friendship?

Aristotle is often credited with the saying: "Misfortune reveals those who are not true friends." This "misfortune" has taught me many things, and I have learned a lot in my own way. It made me aware of the self-respect passed down to me from the old Cossack days. Even if you feel down, do not despair. Even if the odds are against us, we do not have to fit ourselves into the expectations set by others. My origins remind me to overcome hardships by myself, to live as a Ukrainian who is proud of her free spirit.

When I told this to my Japanese friend, they said, "That is amazing. I have a classmate who had a PhD and could not find a decent job, so she killed herself." I was thinking, what a story to tell refugee in search of a job! From my friend's story, I have a renewed feeling that one could be discriminated against in Japan even after earning a PhD. This is especially true when it comes to women. Some of my classmates are working abroad because they could not find a position in Japan even though they had excellent marks and received a doctorate. If they were lucky enough to find a job, they were bullied within the university and had to resign due to worries that they could not cope.

This experience has made me aware of the problems of human nature and the researchers' community. It also taught me the true meaning of friendship. Friendship is not just a kind word, but it is to have the courage to act for the sake of others when they are facing a demanding situation. Now I have fewer friends, but I have more close friends. I am very grateful for that.

(February 13, 2023)

2. The Heroes of Our Time

The Ukrainian Way of Democracy

I have been asked a lot recently what kind of person President Volodymyr Zelenskyy is. However, I do not know much about him since I have never met him in person. In fact, I have never seen any comedy shows or movies in which Zelenskyy appeared, because my preferences are a little different.

I did not vote for him during the presidential election. I could not vote for him because I was in the USA, but I did not plan to vote for him either. When he was elected, I got a phone call from a friend who was in the same university in the US, and she said, "This is terrible! What is going to happen now? He had no experience in politics but got elected thinking it was a game." I remember that time very well.

I got the big news from that friend, who was often posting on social networks. Though it was an interesting way of doing things, I just thought he knew what he had to do to win people's hearts.

When I went back to Kyiv from the USA and visited the countryside, I was talking with an old lady, and this topic came up. She said, "Isn't it good? He would be different from the politicians we had before," which reminded me of the "ee ja nai ka" (meaning "isn't it good") that occurred in Japan at the end of the Edo period (1603-1868). This movement was in fact a demand for changes, carried out in the form of carnivalesque dances, which started in Kyoto and led to the Meiji Restoration.

Surely, it is understandable that people want someone "different from the politicians we had before." Objectively speaking, Ukrainian politics is confusing. It is hard to believe that those who started the Orange Revolution against President Viktor Yanukovych, who tried to falsify the results of the 2004 presidential election, voted 4 years later in 2008 for Yanukovych. Do they have a bad memory?

Nevertheless, some people believe in giving others a second chance and observing how they perform. This reflects the

Ukrainian approach to democracy, where there is a fundamental lack of trust in those in power. Politicians and bureaucrats are met with skepticism from the moment they assume office. In essence, from the Cossacks time in Ukrainian mentality (not like in other post-Soviet countries) power is not granted permanently but is delegated for a limited time so that the public can evaluate whether those in charge are carrying out their responsibilities effectively.

Moreover, the general idea of the masses is that to be in power is too much trouble and they do not want to be involved in policy making. They want whoever is willing to hold power to wield it properly on their behalf. Looking back at the past presidents, after Leonid Kravchuk, who was the leader of the Communist Party, many of them were of the local elite or came from the industrial communities. Leonid Kuchma worked at the rocket factory in Dnipro, Viktor Yanukovych was from Donetsk, Viktor Yushchenko, an economist from Kyiv, and Petro Poroshenko, a confectionery billionaire. However, all of them became president only after the age of 50, being the part of the older generation.

According to a recent study by economic historian Nataliya Kibita[26], since the Soviet era, Kyiv has been a cultural capital with little economic influence. Instead, the coal-producing eastern part and industrial city Dnipro, which produces machinery and rockets, had the money, ability, and confidence to communicate directly with the Communist Party headquarters in Moscow, as well as with relevant ministries. Therefore, even in peacetime, when they were faced with tough decisions, those in the southeast did not wait for instructions from Kyiv but made their decisions by themselves. We can also see it in the current war. The mayors of Dnipro, Kharkiv and Mykolaiv did not wait for orders from the capital.

---

26   I met Nataliya in Harvard in the fall of 2018 and listened to several of her presentations. Recently she published a book. For more see Natalia Kibita, "The Institutional Foundations of Ukrainian Democracy: Power Sharing, Regionalism, and Authoritarianism" (Oxford University Press, 2024).

President Elected as a Result of Voting for the Opposition Candidate

President Volodymyr Zelenskyy was born into an intellectual family not in the capital, but in Kryvyi Rih, an industrial town in the central part of the country. From an early age he was independent and ambitious. He became the leader of a comedy team that appeared on the Russian entertainment show "KVN" (Club of the Cheerful and Quick-witted) and competed with teams from Russia and other countries. He attracted so much attention that he received an offer to move to Moscow, which he turned down, and instead had success in Ukraine, where he established a company with his university friends and produced TV shows and movies.

Considering his methods and path to success, he is living up to the proverb that describes the Ukrainian spirit: "The only help you can give is to leave me alone." The contemporary Ukrainian writer and stage playwright Les Podervyansky expressed the same sentiments in slightly strong terms which I am afraid I cannot quote in a book, because it might be read by children. But basically, it means let the spirit of freedom repel the forces of domination. Do not stand in my way, as I will tackle everything and advance on my own. This may describe the course of Ukrainian politics since the collapse of the Soviet Union. Paraphrasing the title of the book of another Ukrainian writer Oksana Zabuzhko, we can also call it "Let my people go". Zelenskyy, who is a self-made, successful businessperson, must have thought that the times had changed and that he could apply his model of success in politics as well.

When I asked my friends in Kyiv what kind of people voted for Zelenskyy, they answered that most of the supporters were small businesspeople who owned, for instance, retail stores or were taxi drivers. Most of them were from middle-class and lower-class backgrounds, making a living on their own merits. It was easy to understand. He won in all regions except for Lviv in the western part of the country. As for the age groups, 80 percent of those who voted for him were young people under 30.

Seventy five to eighty two percent of the voters did not have a university degree, but rather a high school or vocational school diploma, or junior college degree.

In addition, only 6 percent of the voters had made up their minds who they would vote for by the day of the election. They were fed up with the current politicians and considered voting a game. According to sociologist Iryna Bekeshkina[27], people did not actively choose the candidate they would support, but rather voted for the one they did not dislike, especially during the runoff. Since he won the election in this way, perhaps even Zelenskyy himself did not think he would win. He might have been more troubled than happy with his victory, but nobody knows for sure except for him.

Tracing Transformation Through Speeches

Two years after Volodymyr Zelenskyy was elected president, Russia invaded. War broke out and everyone wondered what would happen now: would he just hand over the country, would he run away? Everyone was anxious. Many people were skeptical about Zelenskyy, who had no previous experience as a politician and had seriously studied the Ukrainian language only after becoming president. For this reason, when the invasion started, the regions did not wait for orders from Kyiv and tried to cope with the situation on their own. Kharkiv, Dnipro and Mykolaiv each formed a local territorial defense force.

However, a surprise awaited them. Zelenskyy did not run anywhere but stayed in Kyiv and kept fighting. Last winter there was a joke among the young people that together with the surface-to-air system, or "Javelins," that were delivered from abroad, courage was delivered to the government offices in Kyiv. It was a pleasant joke that brought tears to my eyes.

More than a year has passed since the beginning of the Russian invasion. During this period, both the popular attitude to

---

27 https://dif.org.ua/article/khto-ti-vibortsi-yaki-obrali-zelenskogo-ta-golosuvali-za-poroshenka-sotsiologi-dali-kharakteristiki-elektoratam-obokh-kandidativ

Zelenskyy and Zelenskyy himself have changed dramatically. He has always been a man from the entertainment sphere and is good at presenting himself. This was confirmed to be a crucial skill in the midst of the ongoing war. In order to see the changes in Zelenskyy and his growth as a politician, let us trace the shifts in his speeches over the past year.

On February 19th, 2022, five days prior to the Russian invasion, Zelenskyy attended the Munich Security Conference and said, "Ukraine wants peace, Europe wants peace, the world does not want to fight, Russia does not want to attack. That means someone is lying. This is no longer an assumption," he said, strongly criticizing the countries that were guarantors of the Budapest Memorandum[28]. Although his use of strong language drew criticism, the war started shortly thereafter, and it turned out that he was right in his outlook.

On the morning of February 24th, the day of the invasion, he said, "Please, do not panic. We are strong. We can win. Because we are Ukrainians." It was only 6 a.m., and he was dressed formally in a shirt, jacket and was clean-shaven.

On the evening of the day of the invasion, he stood in front of the Office of the President, surrounded by Prime Minister Denys Shmyhal, head of the Presidential Administration Andriy Yermak, head of the party "Sluga narodu" (Servant of the People) in Ukrainian Supreme Council Davyd Arakhamiya and advisor to the president Mykhailo Podolyak. He delivered a message lasting a mere dozen seconds in which he said, "We are all here. Our soldiers and citizens are here. We are all staying here. To defend our independence and our country. We are not going to change our decision." It was impressive. He will go down in history as the president who said, "I need ammunition, not a ride (to evacuate)." This line became famous and was used in pop culture. The song "Not a ride, but ammunition" was also popular.

---

28 A Memorandum of Understanding of 1994 in which the USA, the UK, and Russia promised Ukraine the integrity of its borders in exchange for the renunciation of nuclear weapons.

On March 8th, in a video address to the British House of Commons, the President quoted Winston Churchill's words during World War II: "We shall fight on the beaches, we shall fight on the landing grounds, we shall fight in the fields and in the streets, we shall fight in the hills." He then continued, "I would like to add something as well. We will fight in the mountains, on the Kalmius and Dnipro rivers. We shall never surrender." After this speech, Zelenskyy was likened to Churchill.

Until that moment, he had been ridiculed for being a former actor in a TV drama series, but now everyone could see how he had grown as a person and a politician. When I think of presidents, who were formerly actors, I think of Reagan in the United States. In his first term as president, he faced the Afghan War and returned to the era of the East-West confrontation known as the New Cold War. In the spring of 1983, Reagan called the USSR an "evil empire". This is an accurate observation, and it is also relevant to the current invasion.

Online Address to Japan

On March 23rd, 2022, Zelenskyy delivered an online speech in the National Diet of Japan. It was the first time that a foreign Head of state addressed the Diet online. "Our capitals are separated by a distance of 8193 kilometers [...] But what is the distance between our feelings of freedom? Between our desires to live? Between our aspirations for peace? On February 24th, I did not see any distance [...] Because you immediately came to our aid. And I'm grateful to you for that." "You were the first in Asia to put real pressure on Russia to restore peace, who supported the sanctions against Russia and I urge you to continue to do so." "We have similar values with you despite the huge distance between our countries. A distance that doesn't really exist because we have equally warm hearts."

On May 9th, Ukraine's ex-Victory Day, with the destroyed apartment building in Borodianka near Kyiv in the background, the President stated, "Ukraine knows colorless spring." He emphasized that our generation did not expect to experience again the suffering of World War II 77 years after its end, but that its tragedy was being repeated.

On May 17th, Zelenskyy delivered an online speech at the opening ceremony of the Cannes Film Festival. As a former actor, I am sure he would have liked to participate in that festival in a different way. But ironically, fate has forced him to speak as the leader of a war-torn country.

In his speech on August 24th, Independence Day, he said: "The free people of independent Ukraine! We are facing this day in different places. Someone is in the trenches and dugouts, in tanks and IFVs, at sea and in the air. Fighting for independence on the frontline. Someone is on the road, in cars, trucks and trains. Fighting for independence by delivering what is necessary to those on the frontline. And someone is on a smartphone or on a computer, fighting for independence by raising funds so that those on the road have something to bring to those on the frontline."

In a video message to the Venice International Film Festival on August 31st, he showed pictures of 358 children who died in the invasion, describing it as "a drama based on a true story" and "not 120 minutes, but 189 days of terror."

I was very much impressed by his speech to the US Congress on December 22nd. It was the first foreign visit for him since the beginning of the Russian invasion. The members of Congress stood up and applauded warmly, and many Ukrainians, who tend to look at politicians dispassionately, cried when they watched this speech. Zelenskyy emphasized that support for Ukraine's freedom is support for having a future: "Ukraine never asked the American soldiers to fight on our land instead of us. I assure you that Ukrainian soldiers can perfectly operate American tanks and planes themselves."

In his New Year 2023 message, the Ukrainian President asked Russia, "Do you still think we are "one people"?" This speech also shows the free spirit of Ukraine, which would rather be without gas, electricity, water, and food than to be with Russia. "The only help you can do is leave us alone," which means that we are able to stand on our own, so please leave us alone and let us do what we want to do.

When the President visited the UK for the first time on February 8th, 2023, and addressed Parliament, he first thanked the UK for its continuous support for Ukraine since the very first day of the invasion. He pointed out that the people of both countries have the spirit of defeating evil embedded in their traditions. He emphasized that Ukrainians have a free spirit but lack "wings to be free," or airplanes, and called for their support.

Zelensky's oratory and expressive power at that time were highly regarded in the United Kingdom. A week later, when I visited Churchill Museum and Cabinet War Rooms, the building where Churchill and his team had taken refuge during World War II, a volunteer who showed me around said to me, "Your president is young and smart." Indeed, everyone is paying attention to Zelenskyy and assessing him from a historical point of view.

Becoming Represented in Popular Culture

Zelenskyy, who used to be highly criticized for his Ukrainian pronunciation, has improved over the past years. There is a video on TikTok, where he could not remember a word in Russian and is asking the staff to remind him of the translation, and Ukrainians received it well. Two years ago, it would have been unthinkable that he could forget a Russian word.

As we look back on the political history of the Soviet Union, many politicians were not good at making speeches, except for the last president Mikhail Gorbachev. However, his speeches and actions did not match with each other, so he was not popular inside the country. Especially after the Chornobyl nuclear accident, he did not visit Ukraine for 3 years, so Ukrainians had a strong distrust toward him.

Among the presidents of independent Ukraine, only Leonid Kravchuk was a good speaker. His Ukrainian was charming because he had used it daily since he was a child. However, he was a man who put his own position first and was not a person of action. Viktor Yushchenko and Petro Poroshenko, who were good Ukrainian speakers, both differed in their own words and deeds. On the contrary, Zelenskyy has gained a lot of fans over the past year, even among his haters. His words and actions have matched. His ability to speak Ukrainian has improved and his speeches show his growth as a politician and as a person. He has gained respect at once.

Unlike previous politicians, he is a young president who wears a khaki T-shirt and smiles with a tired face, without looking arrogant and power-hungry. As a former comedian, he is becoming more popular by making fun of his enemies. He is also Jewish, which makes him a more representative leader for a modern, multi-ethnic Ukraine.

He is an easily relatable president, which is why he also came to be represented in pop culture. Not only are there T-shirts with Zelenskyy printed on them, but there are also songs about him. A rapper Misha Pravilniy wrote such a song. In the lyrics, the president is considered a peer of his generation and is referred to by the nickname Vova. This alone shows that everyone finds something congenial in the president, even though he should normally be addressed by at least his patronymic along with his personal name. In the song "Hello, Vova," the lyrics are as follows: "I don't care much about politics. For me, this entire system is rotten," "Come on, Mr. President, don't give up, as we too won't be giving up. We believe in you, we believe in our army, see you at the exit (of this movie)."[29]

It is rare for such lyrics to appear in Ukraine. As I mentioned earlier, in Ukraine there has always been a lack of trust in politicians and those in power. From the day they are elected, people begin to doubt and observe them. So, as for Zelenskyy, no one can guarantee what will happen later, even if he is praised now. But at this moment, he is the best president we have ever had.

(February 18, 2023)

---

29 https://www.youtube.com/watch?v=5dlNDhcPq_s

3. Taras Shevchenko, National Poet

Three Poets, whose Portraits are on the Banknotes

The other day, one of my friends in Japan asked me why there is no "national poet" in Japan like there is in Ukraine. Indeed, it is true. In Japan there was Matsuo Basho in the Edo period, Ishikawa Takuboku in the Meiji period, and Shuntaro Tanikawa in the modern period, who are famous as poets expressing the soul of Japanese people, however they are not called "national poets." Perhaps it is because there was no definition of nation at that time, but I am not sure.

In Ukraine, there have been outstanding poets during each historical period. Taras Shevchenko in the 19th century, Ivan Franko and Lesya Ukrainka in the 20th century, Lina Kostenko and Vasyl Symonenko in the 1960s during the Soviet era. Nowadays there are such poets as Serhiy Zhadan. All of them are representative poets of their times, and Ukrainians have a special affection for poetry and poets.

In the summer of 2017, my friend from Japan came to visit me and we went to the Ukrainian Art Museum located a short walk from Independence Square. Our goal was to see the first floor with the exhibition of Cossack icons and the second floor with impressionist paintings done by Ukrainians who studied in Paris. However, we found out that the exhibition was closed that day for a poetry reading by Serhiy Zhadan. About 100 people had gathered at the venue, waiting for the poet, who was running late. The artist himself is a poet and writer in his late forties and the front man of a punk rock band "Zhadan and the Dogs". The band's lyrics are radical, but Zhadan writes sensitive poems about love and has many female fans. My Japanese friend was surprised to see so many people gathered. They said they could not imagine such a large crowd at a poet reading in Japan. I remember my thought that in Ukraine, especially at Zhadan's reading, it is considered usual.

I think that the position of poetry and poets in Ukrainian society can be seen through Ukrainian banknotes. I will introduce to you some portraits on the banknotes. On the front of the 1000-hryvnia banknote is Volodymyr Vernadsky, founder and first head of the Ukrainian Academy of Sciences, and on the back is the building of the Academy itself. The 500-hryvnia banknote has the philosopher Hryhoriy Skovoroda on the front and the building of the Kyiv-Mohyla Academy on the reverse. The 200-hryvnia banknote shows the poet Lesya Ukrainka and there is a picture of the castle of her hometown Lutsk on the back. The 100-hryvnia banknote shows Taras Shevchenko on the front and the building of the Kyiv University named after him on the back. The 50-hryvnia banknote depicts the President and historian of the independent Ukrainian Republic of 1918, Mykhailo Hrushevsky, and the building of its Central Council.

Among smaller denominations, the 20-hryvnia banknote shows the poet Ivan Franko and the opera theater in Lviv, the 10-hryvnia banknote shows Ivan Mazepa, a Cossack leader who fought with Sweden against Russia, and the Uspensky Cathedral of the Kyiv-Pechersk Monastery. The denominations of 1, 2, and 5 hryvnias were previously in the form of banknotes, however recently got fully converted to the coin form. The 5-hryvnia coin shows Bohdan Khmelnytsky, a Cossack leader who negotiated with the Russians in Pereiaslav in 1654, and the church in the Subotiv village, where he is buried. On the 2-hryvnia coin Yaroslav the Wise, Grand Prince of Kyiv, and the St. Sophia Cathedral are depicted, and, finally, the 1-hryvnia banknote has Volodymyr the Great and the part of Kyiv he built.

In other words, we can divide those people into the following groups: scholars, poets, Cossacks, and politicians. The fact that there are three poets on the banknotes shows the high status of poets in Ukraine.

Taras Shevchenko

Besides his portrait on the 100-hryvnia banknote, monuments of Taras Shevchenko are in every Ukrainian city. Shevchenko was born in 1814 and died early, in 1861 at the age of 47. He was born into a peasant family in central Ukraine, but his ancestors were Cossacks. When the Cossack state was crushed and incorporated into the Russian Empire, the Ukrainian ex-Cossacks also became peasants.

His mother died when he was 9 years old, and his father remarried. However, his stepmother neglected him, and so he moved to live with relatives. He taught himself painting while helping with church work. At the age of 14, he was hired as an errand boy for a landowner, who took him to Vilnius, Lithuania, and other places, expanding his world. The landowner wanted to train Shevchenko to be his private painter, so in 1831, when he was 17 years old, he sent him to learn the art of painting in St. Petersburg, the capital of the Russian Empire. It was around this time that he began to write poetry.

In St. Petersburg he met Ukrainian painters, writers and poets who appreciated his work and decided to buy him out of serfdom. Shevchenko painted a picture of the poet Vasily Zhukovsky, who at that time was a Russian teacher of the royal family and got the family of the tsar to buy it. Ironically, the Russian royal family was later criticized by a Ukrainian poet who came to great prominence. The remuneration for the painting was used to buy him out, and that is how he was freed from serfdom in 1838.

After that, Shevchenko studied at the Academy of Fine Arts in St. Petersburg for about five years, but secretly continued to write poetry in Ukrainian. He was equally talented both as a painter and as a poet. Perhaps, he had been thinking a lot about his experience as a serf, a shame complex of his village origin, and his national pride. Shevchenko expressed in his poems the life of peasants, which no one had paid attention to before. He could have been famous and lived a long life if he had devoted himself to painting, but he could not help but express himself in poetry.

One of his friends read a poem he had written while at the Academy, which led to the publication of a collection of his poetry. His collection "Kobzar" was published in 1840 with 1000 copies printed and made Shevchenko famous in an instant.

Thoughts he had while living in St. Petersburg, are well expressed in his poem "My Thoughts."

As a child Shevchenko heard many stories about the Cossack period from his grandfather. At that time, the history of Ukraine was told orally, but for the first time he wrote these stories in the beautiful form of poetry, thus elevating the Ukrainian language spoken by the common people to the level of literature. Until then, the Ukrainian language was considered a primitive peasant language, incompatible with literature and poetry. Shevchenko is considered the father of the modern Ukrainian language.

Multiple Arrests and Death

He then was commissioned by the Archaeological Committee to work as a painter of historical monuments and stayed in Ukraine twice. However, in 1847, he was arrested on suspicion of involvement with the Brotherhood of Saints Cyril and Methodius, a movement of Ukrainian intellectuals in favor of transforming the empire into a federation of Slavic peoples, ideally with liberal political freedoms, and a special role for Ukraine. Because of his poem "Dream," which ironically describes the Empress of the Russian Empire, he was exiled to a remote border guard post. Shevchenko himself must have known that writing and publishing his poems in Ukrainian would have alerted the government.

For the record, Mykola Hohol (1809-1852, Nikolai Gogol in Russian), who was 5 years older than Shevchenko, was also born in Ukraine to a family of Cossack origin and lived in St. Petersburg. However unlike Shevchenko, he wrote his works about Ukraine in Russian. Although he hated St. Petersburg and always wanted to return to Ukraine, he continued to write in Russian, perhaps because it was more convenient for him, or maybe he wanted to blend in with Russian society. Or simply it sold better.

Literary critic and historian Serhii Efremov describes Hohol, who was a playwright, novelist, and poet, as a man of "two souls."[30] Typical of Ukrainian intellectuals of the time, he was

---

30 Serhii Efremov. "Miz dvoma dushamy. Mykola Hohol" (Kyiv, 1909).

bilingual, speaking Russian in formal settings and thinking in Ukrainian. He wrote in Russian about the traditions and songs of the Ukrainian countryside. In a sense, he tried to globalize Ukrainian culture, customs, and traditions, but the Russian Empire digested them all and presented them as Russian culture.

Shevchenko respected Hohol. Taras accepted Mykola's sarcastic remarks and wrote to him in his poem "To Hohol":

> You laugh full deep while
> I must weep,
> My great and mighty friend![31]

Shevchenko continued to write poetry even in exile. In his poem "The Cherry Orchard" he describes an ideal everyday life in Ukraine. It is a scene of a peaceful and happy family eating together in a cherry blossom garden. Like the poem describes, in Ukraine it is still an everyday scene to have a meal at the table under a tree in the garden in spring and summer. Every Ukrainian who reads this poem thinks of their grandmother's house, their own parents' house, or a country house where they spend their summer.

From 1850 to 1857, Shevchenko was exiled to Kos-Aral, in present-day Kazakhstan, where the climate was harsh and reading and writing were forbidden, which caused him great hardship. Even so, he continued to write poetry secretly on a piece of paper small enough to be hidden in his long boots. The soldiers guarding him took pity on him and turned a blind eye.

When Tsar Nicholas I of Russia died in 1855, Shevchenko's friends did their best to have him released, and 2 years later he was finally freed. He returned to St. Petersburg and worked as a painter and printmaker, living in poverty, and preparing to publish an anthology of poems. However, he was arrested again in 1859 and died two years later.

---

31   *Translated by C.H. Andrusyshen and Watson Kirkconnellin:* The Poetical Works of Taras Shevchenko. The Kobzar. Translated from the Ukrainian by C.H. Andrusyshen and Watson Kirkconnell. Published for the Ukrainian Canadian Committee by University of Toronto Press, 1964. Toronto and Buffalo. Printed in Canada, reprinted 1977, p. 181-182.

Shevchenko had already authored a poem titled "Testament" in 1845, before he was arrested, while he was traveling in Ukraine. After his death, as he says in the poem, he was buried on a hill by the Dnipro River in Kaniv, now Cherkasy region. When the coffin was transported from St. Petersburg, the government had to provide tight security with police officers to prevent any political demonstrations. Even after his death, the poet was considered dangerous.

People Still Read Shevchenko

Taras Shevchenko's poetry is indispensable when we think about the national independence of Ukrainian people. He wrote many wonderful poems about life, happiness and misfortune, destiny, motherhood and pregnancy out of wedlock. They can be read today with the same relevance, regardless of the historical period.

Since Shevchenko had a tragic life and was arrested many times by the government, during the Soviet era he was presented as a "poet of the revolution" as the only poems that were featured were those filled with anger toward the ruling class. However, he did not write only social poetry. He also authored many romantic poems. Shevchenko considered love a significant part of life, and many of his poems are dedicated to various women. Even in prison, he wrote: "Without the one you love, you will spend your days without pleasure." In many of his poems, he depicted Ukrainian landscapes and rich nature as essential for peace of mind.

In the USSR, the supporters of independence cherished Taras Shevchenko's poems. There is a bronze statue of Shevchenko made in the Soviet era, standing in front of the Kyiv National University. It was only a token gesture by the government, however, every year on March 9th, his birthday, flowers were laid on the statue by the activists, and it was always subject to a police crackdown against "Ukrainian nationalism." The Soviet government was well aware of the profound influence of his poetry.

The Ukrainian poet was introduced to Japan by members of the leftist school of thought. In the 1960s, a poet and rural activist named Shibuya Teisuke introduced Taras Shevchenko for the first time. However, he didn't translate any of Shevchenko's poems and was more interested in his life and struggle against governmental oppressions. In 1993, Professor Etsuko Fujii, a scholar of Ukrainian literature translated the book directly from Ukrainian (previously it was a retranslation of Russian and English language versions), and has been published several books since then. "Taras Shevchenko Poetry Collection: Kobzar" published in 2018 is a beautiful book with comments by Etsuko Fujii, who translated it, and it is a reference book not only for a deeper understanding of Shevchenko's works but also for Ukrainian linguistics and area studies.

In fact, when Etsuko Fujii and I co-translated and published "A Short Anthology of Contemporary Ukrainian Literature" in 2005, we received a letter from a reader. The reader asked why we did not translate cheerful uplifting works, since our book was full of gloomy and dark pieces, so contrary to the vivid landscapes that impressed him when he visited Kyiv. However, if we look at the literary works Ukraine has produced in the last hundred years or so, only a few of them are cheerful. This is because literature reflects the destiny of a country, and unfortunately Ukraine has had a difficult history.

After the War Broke Out

The poetry of Taras Shevchenko has been part of the school curriculum since Soviet times, despite the limited number of works covered. During the Orange Revolution in 2004, I had a chance to read it again. At that time, graffiti with Shevchenko's face appeared, with a hat like that of Che Guevara in Cuba, and the names of those two were mixed into the title "She Guevara." It became a symbol of courage. The same phenomenon occurred again after the Russian invasion. Many inspiring posters of Shevchenko fighting appeared, and I was encouraged by them. Meanwhile, since he is such a strong anti-Russian symbol, his statues and school portraits have been vandalized all over the Russian-occupied territories.

Recently, Ukrainians often cite the following line from Shevchenko's poem "The Caucasus":

> Keep fighting—you are sure to win!
> God helps you in your fight!
> For fame and freedom march with you,
> And right is on your side![32]

In addition, there are other active Ukrainian poets. Serhiy Zhadan from Kharkiv, mentioned at the beginning of this section, remained in the city, helping the local defense forces, then travelling abroad and fundraising money for the army, then donating the profits from the sale of his books at auctions to refugees and the army, and talking to foreign media. Andriy Lyubka, a young poet and writer from Uzhhorod, a town located near the Hungarian border, with the donation from people bought 130 cars and donated them to the army. He concentrated so much on his volunteer activities that could not write a single line of a new piece of work.

One may have the impression that poets and writers write their works in a quiet and calm environment, such as a library. In Ukraine, however, depending on the period, this was not always the case.

(February 22, 2023)

---

[32] Translated by *John Weir* in Taras Shevchenko. Selected poetry Kiev, "Dnipro", 1977, p. 187 - 197.

4. War and Business

Various Businesses in the Wartime

Especially in times of war, we need basic things like food, clothing and shelter. People must take care of the elderly and children and earn money in order to do so. You may think that business might have stopped because of the war. But this was not the case in Ukraine. It is actually fascinating to observe consumer behavior and business practices in wartime Ukraine and how business owners approach these issues.

When the invasion started, people were desperately evacuating their families to the west or out of the country. However, the first month was especially difficult for those who ran their own businesses. It is the responsibility of management to protect their employees, equipment, and premises. War is an exemption clause, so insurance will not cover any damage. This is true for personal belongings, but it is especially true for corporate property. Therefore, many companies were desperate to protect themselves, and many were evacuated to the west.

According to the statistics of the Ukrainian business sector, a quarter of companies are bankrupt due to the invasion. Even if they did not go bankrupt, many of them had layoffs. I have heard many such stories during the past year. On the other hand, there were also stories of CEOs who have not laid off a single employee. All the companies were desperate to resume their operations, first protecting their companies and employees until April, and then trying to start their businesses again. Many companies were also struggling with how to secure human resources as their employees were drafted or left the country. According to the European Business Association, 28 percent of the companies were back in business as of April last year and 47 percent in June. The next step was to work hard to regain the pre-war situation and profits.

However, even during wartime, demand has increased, and sales have grown in some sectors. For example, portable foodstuffs with a long shelf life. Companies that used to make dried fruit have expanded their product range to include foods such as jerky.

In many cases, office workers lost their jobs and started their own businesses. There was a person who opened a store in western Ukraine when they evacuated to their parents' house in the village, after realizing that there was no coffee shop with good internet access, good coffee, or a bomb shelter.

The number of companies that make military-style clothes has also increased. Due to war, people cannot afford luxuries, but there are many people who want a khaki-colored jumper like the one that President Zelenskyy is always wearing, and that is where the business comes in. In fact, the military fashion company that Zelenskyy wears has also evacuated to the west and continues its business. The company's young owner has been influential in changing the local apparel culture. They are incorporating new management methods learned from abroad into the old artisan culture.

Some companies have emerged to build reliable bomb shelters for people to hide in the event of an air raid warning. They team up with construction companies to build proper shelters with Wi-Fi in newly built apartments. There is also a need for companies that make construction related products and tools and can build and repair sturdy buildings.

Automobile repair shops and equipment and parts manufacturers are also increasing their sales. In times of war, people realized that automobiles are indispensable not only for the military, but also for civilians. Since they cannot buy new cars, there is an increasing demand for the sale and maintenance of used cars.

Since June of 2022, customs duties are no longer imposed on exports to the EU, so the number of companies exporting goods, especially food stuffs, has also increased. As a result, according to the trade statistics of Ukraine in 2022, trade with the EU accounted for about 40 percent of the total. The number of consulting firms acting as intermediaries for the sale of goods abroad has also increased. There are many Ukrainians who have fled to other countries to investigate the local business environment and turn it into a business opportunity.

Most of the evacuees are women and children, but most Ukrainian women take the initiative and care for their families and children. They want to improve their lives economically and secure a safe environment. For example, one of my acquaintances who evacuated with her infant to Spain was originally a nutritionist, and in almost two months she set up an English website and expanded her global customer base. On the other hand, she got tired of taking care of her kid and found herself anxious about her family in Kyiv, to the extent that she was unable to rest. Therefore, she opened a beauty salon in Barcelona with a variety of services. She rented a beautiful space of 100 square meters and began to operate there with a hairdresser, a nail artist, and a massage therapist, all of whom were Ukrainian refugees. Opening a new workplace is a good thing, as it provides a place to earn money and a place for everyone to get together.

On the other hand, there are many companies that have relocated to the western part of the country and started completely new businesses. In times of war, the consumption of some goods has even been increasing. Among such goods are food, baby products, and toys. As in any country, Ukrainian parents care about their children, so there is a great business opportunity to expand the market for baby products. Many parents try to ensure the safety, education, and entertainment of their children suffering from various hardships during the war. Private kindergartens and schools with bomb shelters are also emerging.

Ukrainians treasure not only the birthdays of their children, but also of adults, and even in wartime many Ukrainians try to hold birthday parties for their kids. Such needs have led to an increase in the number of event companies that help organize such parties.

Ukrainian parents are also enthusiastic about their children's studies. Online consumption has been growing since the pandemic. However, especially in wartime, displaced children continue to take online lessons in foreign languages, mathematics, painting, music, dance, singing, and sometimes even sports. In the three years since the pandemic the online learning system has fully developed.

It is War, so We Must not Rest?

Another surprisingly large market is recreation. With the ongoing war, there are few opportunities for people to take a break and truly relax. In this context, items that can be described as "healing" or "petit rest" tend to sell well.

For example, there is a service that allows you to take a break for three hours. It is a business that offers packages for those who have leave from the army, or for those who are always too nervous to rest due to power outages or air raid warnings, to peacefully rest for a while. Examples include a three-hour Kyiv tours, massage packages, saunas, nail services, renting a private movie theater of a size of small room, and so on. Among longer tours, day trips to the countryside are popular as well.

Despite the variety of services offered, there is still a conviction that people should not rest in wartime. However, psychologists also emphasize the need for a change of pace and rest to prevent our minds from burning out even in times of war. There is no need to feel guilty about it. But since everyone has that conviction, the media, psychologists and celebrities are trying to change that social norm by talking about their experiences.

Nowadays it is often said that even if we are convinced that we should not laugh, rest, or travel during war, it will not benefit anyone, and we will not win the war in such a way. First of all, we need to take diligent care of our bodies and minds. It is precisely because of the reality of war that we should live our daily lives to the fullest.

If you still feel guilty, you can donate to those who are in a worse situation than yours. In Ukraine there are many such people around. Colleagues who voluntarily enlisted in the army, a son of a friend, a husband of an acquaintance, etc. It is surely not easy for the elderly who live alone or for people with disabilities.

We need to change the pace and space a little to divert our thoughts from the reality of war. It is also recommended to be in touch with nature, by fishing, riding bicycles, etc. If you cannot go to the countryside, you can decorate your house with flowers or grow plants. I bought tulips in early spring last year, put them in a vase and enjoyed watching them open every day.

It has become a challenge to go abroad, as Ukraine is a no-fly zone. Nevertheless, there are people who cross the Polish, Slovak, and Hungarian borders either by car or by train from Kyiv. From Warsaw, Bratislava or Budapest, you can fly anywhere. But unfortunately, it takes a long time. One of my students went to Italy for a three-day trip and said it took them an entire day just to get on the plane in Poland. She recalled good times when she could easily get on a plane, because it takes only forty minutes by taxi to get to Terminal D of Boryspil International Airport (incidentally, it was built with a Japanese yen loan) from the center of Kyiv.

Many people are unable to relax because stress becomes so ingrained in their bodies that the muscles in their necks and shoulders have become stiffened. Doctors recommend physical activity, so many gyms have reopened since the spring of 2022. Since October, the attacks on Kyiv's infrastructure have continued, but people were still training in the dark with a flashlight on their heads. Many people have bought hats with electric lights attached to them.

Crisis Sells Bread

I have a friend who runs with her brother a group of companies in western Ukraine producing yeast and pet food. I am glad to see that they are doing their best to overcome various problems after the Russian invasion. However, there are many painful stories that are not reported in the newspapers.

She refused to believe that there would be a war until the very end. Nevertheless, she started to prepare for it little by little in December 2021 when the international media started to make a fuss. While thinking that she was taking the rumors close to heart, she prepared a shelter just in case, since 300 people work for her company. She conducted an evacuation drill for workers in case of an air raid alert with the hope they would never use it. Besides, my friend really likes Japanese business philosophy calls *"kaizen"* and according to it principles tries not to keep a stock, but just in case, she stocked up two months' worth of ingredients and food. In addition, she stocked up on everything she could buy in Ukraine for her company — such as nitric and sulfuric acids, which are manufactured in the eastern part of the country, as well as materials for packaging. She felt safe for the time being because she could manufacture for two months without being affected by the war. When the invasion started, only two or three people had to evacuate.

In February, they received an offer from a Polish logistics and sales representative to take in the children of their employees, along with their parents. At first no one wanted to evacuate, but as the number of air raid alarms increased and missiles began to fly, more people were willing to go. In the end, several hundred people were evacuated to Poland. The president of one of their Polish business partners allowed six people to live in his house. It was a small town in the countryside, an the children were allowed to attend classes at school and go sightseeing on weekends. Their help came in a very natural way, and the Ukrainian staff were all incredibly grateful.

Missiles also hit the company's premises. However, they were safe because it hit a sturdy wall built in the Austro-Hungarian period. It was a missile made in the Soviet era.

The company has three factories in different parts of Ukraine. Besides the one in western Ukraine, the other two are located in Kharkiv and Kryvyi Rih. At the beginning of the invasion, these two factories could not operate, but the yeast for baking sold exceptionally well. As it was during the pandemic, this product seems to sell well when people have a keen sense of crisis. Apparently, more people buy it to bake bread at home, fearing that they may not be able to go to the store to buy it. On the contrary, in times of peace, people feel more secure and are more concerned about their health, which seems to reduce the consumption of bread.

These two factories have resumed production, and half of their products are for export. In addition, the depreciation of the hryvnia a year ago happened. In spite of the demanding situation, none of the export partners stopped doing business with them. Certainly, they had a plan B in case production stopped, but no one said that trade should stop in the event of war. Croatian and German customers in particular were wonderful, and the export volume increased. Croatians encouraged them by saying, "We have experienced war, too. A company that does well in times of peace will do well even in times of war."

The Russian Factory was Sold Off for a Couple of Dollars

A few years ago, the company noticed that the consumption of bread was beginning to decline, so they decided to enter the biobusiness to see if there were other uses for yeast. They have a research and development (R&D) department for biotechnology. When the invasion started, the company first closed its website because of the risk of becoming a target of attack. Then they secretly donated money to the army. Once a year, in the spring, the company announces that it will donate 20 percent of the sales of one of its yeast brands to the army, and the money donated amounted to 4-5 million hryvnias.

A year prior to the invasion, they borrowed half of the construction costs to build a new factory. After the invasion, construction stopped for several weeks. The original plan was to open in the summer of 2022, so in mid-March they decided to resume construction as they saw no point in stopping. My friend strongly believes in the future of Ukraine and that is the company policy as well, so she decided to resume the works. The opening was scheduled for the end of February 2023, and although she invited partners from outside of Ukraine, no one came because of the war. Nevertheless, the factory smoothly started its operation.

There are two products made at the new factory. One is a supplement for livestock. With the consumption of bread on the decline, they turned their attention to the livestock industry and created a supplement from yeast that allows chickens, pigs, and cows to gain weight in a natural way. The company now exports its products not only domestically, but also to 24 countries. She plans to expand their sales network to Asia, and in terms of Japan she is considering talking to dairy farmers in Hokkaido.

Another product is seasoning, derived from yeast, which naturally brings out synergy of *umami* flavor. The first samples of this product have been shipped internationally. In the autumn of 2022, the first exhibition outside the country after the invasion was held in Paris. There was no "This is a product of Ukraine and I do not want to be involved in politics." On the contrary, the brand "Made in Ukraine" had a positive effect. The brand effect alone will probably not last for a long time; the quality of the product must be good. To sell probiotic yeast and livestock supplements in Europe, a permit was required and successfully obtained. The debt to build the new facility was paid off on time. The company continues to pay salaries to its 300 employees, and no one was fired.

However, the air raid alerts have reduced the efficiency of the work. Yeast must be packaged on time because it ferments when it comes in contact with the air. Sometimes it is not possible to evacuate to a shelter when an air raid alert is issued. However, sales and EBITDA (Earnings Before Interest, Taxes, Depreciation and Amortization) have increased during the past year.

In fact, this company had a factory in Russia. However, in 2015, she ceded it to a company she had jointly invested in with a Canadian company. On March 10th, 2022, she sold her remaining share to the Canadian joint venture partner for about US$100. Apparently, she felt compelled to discard such a repugnant asset. The joint venture partner told her that she could do whatever she wanted with half of the profits for the next five years, but she wanted to give it up anyway.

The children of my entrepreneur friend are out of the country. She says that sometimes she goes to see them and sometimes they come to visit her. When asked what it is like to do business in this situation, she answers: "I am already used to it". She says she can now distinguish which direction the missiles are coming from, as well as the sounds made by a drone from Belarus and missiles fired from the Caspian Sea.

When I asked her what her source of energy was, she told me it was a swimming pool and gym where she works out with a personal trainer every morning from 7:00am. When I asked her why she goes to the gym if she has sporting equipment at home, she replied, smiling, that she uses it as a shelter, and that exercising alone is boring.

The most difficult time for her was when the internet went down due to a blackout. She felt really anxious. She then bought a battery-powered radio and felt a little relieved. For the first few months, she could not read or watch movies at all, but now she watches movies on Netflix.

The first time she left the country after the invasion, she was shocked to see people relaxing, smiling, and drinking in coffee shops along the seaside. It was painful. She kept asking herself why her country had to suffer.

One male employee worked without a vacation for the first nine months, saying he did not need a day off. The first time he had vacation leave might have been at Christmas. My friend was worried for him as he is the type that does not show his emotions, and she probably realized he was running on adrenaline during these months.

Business Expansion Even in the Midst of War

The sister and brother also make pet food in anticipation of declining sales of yeast for bread. Also, the pandemic has increased the number of people who own dogs and cats because they are lonely at home for long periods of time and need a reason to take a walk. This led to the increase of pet food consumption. In addition, since Russian manufacturers have largely withdrawn from the Ukrainian market since 2014, this was an opportunity for them to increase their market share. The company invested in facilities, introduced new technologies, and developed new products, which led to a significant growth. Now it is a big company, selling pet food to 32 countries and employing 1300 people. During the COVID-19 outbreak, they built a big factory in Lithuania and decided to manufacture in the EU and sell directly to Europe instead of exporting from Ukraine.

As a pet food company, they were committed to providing animals with healthy food and a friendly environment. They even produced a radio program explaining the care of pets and the psychology of animals. Employees often bring their dogs and cats to the company. A campaign "Bring your Pet to work" was launched throughout Ukraine at that time. It is a fascinating and innovative campaign. When the war broke out, the company took care of abandoned dogs and cats and even tried to find new owners for them.

Many internally displaced people moved to western Ukraine, and those of them who used to make food for their dogs on their own switched to commercial pet food. Many pet owners feel sorry for their dogs and cats as pets were displaced as well. They want to buy better food for pets, so the company has increased the production of the premium products. They also export to the USA and Europe.

We can learn a lot from these siblings, who remain upbeat about the future and work hard, even in times of war.

(March 30, 2023)

5. Friends on the Other Side

A Phone Call That Day

I have some Russian friends from a long time ago. They called me at noon on February 24th, but I could not answer. I did not know what to say. One was a businessman in St. Petersburg who had just returned from a business trip abroad that day. He called me when he heard the news on the radio. I did not answer, so he left a voicemail saying: "This is unbelievable. Unbelievable! I am so sorry."

Another friend from my twenties, after I had not answered, left me a short message on a social network asking "Are you safe?" I replied, "I'm fine. Everyone is alive." After that I received: "Be patient. I hope the Russians will not advance beyond the eastern part (of Ukraine)." However, it did not turn out that way.

After that, sometimes I received just one question, "Are you okay?"

In retrospect, there may have been a harbinger in January, just before the war started. I was doing an online interview for a Japanese documentary with an athlete from *that* country. At the end of the interview, he suddenly asked me, "Is it cold in your house?" When I answered that it was warm, he laughed and said, "It will be cold soon because the gas will be turned off." Finally he added: "Be careful when you go outside." When I asked him why, he said, "Kyiv has a lot of radical nationalists these days, renaming big streets to nationalist names. Be careful of them." I replied with a laugh, "No, they don't. We have streets in our city named after famous soccer players and coaches."

I had no idea that only a month later Russians would launch a missile at the apartment building on Lobanovskyy Boulevard named after Valeriy Lobanovskyy, the coach of FC Dynamo Kyiv for almost 20 years (and was also the national coach of the USSR and Ukraine) and destroy its 19th and 20th floors. It was a big shock for me too, because this residential building was built next to the school I went to. When I think about it, there was a military facility there in the Soviet era, when I was a child. When the Soviet Union collapsed, the facility was closed and the land was redeveloped into a nice residential district. I even wondered if they were using Soviet paper maps to launch missiles at Kyiv of 2022 (roughly 30 years later). Maybe it happened because most of the Soviet maps were created during 1970s and only a small portion were made during 1990s.

I still cannot forget the devastation that I felt on February 24th when I saw the videos of a missile flying over the road I used to walk on as a child. I had a feeling that the war might not end soon if they went this far, but I did not want to admit it. By then I had forgotten the conversation we had during the online interview.

All of my Russian friends are men. I have known them for more than 20 years. But ever since the invasion, we do not talk anymore. I do not even feel like talking to them. I do not know their views on the war and I did not want to ruin old friendships, so I let it be for a while. One of them apologized to me at the beginning of March. I replied, "I don't want to talk about this now, so let's talk about it another time" to which he replied, "We may never talk about it again. You will never forgive us, and I will be ashamed. What you went through is too terrible and I cannot remain in a good mood after that. We will not be able to talk afterwards, will we?"

It was a good expression of our feelings. But I felt that our friendship would naturally end if we did not talk.

Views of Ukrainians on Russia

Ukrainian feelings toward Russia and the Russian language have been shaped through a variety of historical and cultural processes. In 1654, the Cossacks led by Bohdan Khmelnytsky (1595-1657) signed a treaty with the Russian Empire guaranteeing them autonomy in order to protect their country. The Cossacks were fighting for nobiliary privileges and Orthodox rights within Poland, and Ivan Vyhovsky (1608-1664) still tried to create a tripartite Commonwealth (Poland-Lithuania-Ruthenia) in 1658, but this failed. Also, the Cossack Hetmanate retained considerable autonomy within Russia until Peter the Great and Catherine the Great started integrating it more tightly with the rest of the empire. This process began in the Great Northern War because Peter the Great was trying to extract resources, while Catherine the Great eventually abolished the Hetmanate and turned it into a set of ordinary gubernias [33] of Russian Empire, which actually became a colony.

However, until recently, many researchers refrained from using the term "colony" because ethnically Russian lands around Moscow did not have self-rule either, and their residents were not treated very well. Also, because unlike in the British or French Empires, there weren't big bodies of water clearly separating the metropole from the colonies. Also, the Russian ruling elite was multiethnic and multiconfessional.

In Right-Bank Ukraine, the imperial government initially worked with the wealthy Polish landowners, while the Cossack leaders (starshyna) of the Left Bank intermarried with Russians and gradually lost their old identity. Probably the Russian term "okrainy" (outskirts or margins, or borderlands) can be useful here, because that is how the imperial government described the areas outside of so called "Core Russia" or "native Russia" (korenniaia Rossiia in Russian). The colonial phase started early in Crimea and Novorossiia under Catherine the Great because its demography and economic structure were being changed through state policies sometimes modeled on British or Spanish ones in the New World, while the other Ukrainian lands entered a colonial arrangement in the second half of the nineteenth century as the government started building railroads and moving raw materials from there to Moscow and St. Petersburg.

As a general definition, a colony is something external to the suzerain state or something that was incorporated during the process of internal colonization, like in the case of Native Americans in the USA or indigenous and enslaved populations in other settler-colonial countries. The Russian Empire viewed its

---

[33] A territorial administrative unit in the Russian Empire, originally introduced by Peter the Great in the early 18th century

colonies as its integral territory, because the empire was geographically contiguous rather than spread over multiple continents divided by oceans and seas, though some places, like Central Asia or the North Caucasus, were clearly more alien than other predominantly Slavic lands. This was a form of taking over neighboring lands and adding them to the territory of Russian empire. The question of whether to consider Ukrainian territories as a colony is connected with the question of whether the Cossack country, or the former Hetmanate, was still considered as autonomous or fully merged into the empire. While the Hetmanate had its own borders and elites, the concept of an ethnographically defined Ukrainian national territory did not really emerge until the 19th century. Also, there was historically a division between the Zaporizhzhian Sich near the Black Sea and the Hetmanate further north. The former was much unrulier and less integrated with Russia prior to the second half of the eighteenth century. Further north lay Sloboda Ukraine, another military buffer zone and borderland settlement project in which the promise of freedom from imperial taxes encouraged Cossacks to establish their homes and defend the frontier from Tatar raids while enabling the Russian state to protect its power southward.

Russia expanded its colonial holdings in Ukraine, the Caucasus, and Central Asia, sending peasants to Siberia as settlers to develop the lands by promising them a good deal. Still, some of them went there also because they were seeking freedom outside of the suppression of political centres.

On the other hand, there were a number of Ukrainian elites who saw annexation as making Ukraine part of a larger power and creating possibilities for career growth. They were actively carving out their own path in Russian society. This is especially true as early as the late 17th and early 18th centuries with the Cossack starshyna who intermarried with Russian nobles and saw the Hetmanate's incorporation as a chance for social mobility and wealth acquisition. This is why, by the time of Nicholas I, Ukrainians were effectively a peasant people whose native elites had undergone Russification, often voluntarily. The Russification of the 19th century, by contrast, was more coercive and theoretically concerned with the whole "Little Russian" population, though Ukrainians and Russians continued to intermarry and Russian was, until very late, the language of culture and science for educated Ukrainians.

Yet, self-proclaimed Ukrainians faced serious limitations on how they could discuss their identity in public, though their "Little Russian" counterparts enjoyed some freedom in this regard provided they did not challenge the governmental line on the existence of a "triune Russian nation". But some did not forget their roots and secretly researched and wrote about them. For example, Mykola Arkas (1853-1899), who worked as a lawyer in the Russian Empire, collected Ukrainian folk songs and wrote a book about Ukrainian history. His "History of Ukraine" was published in St. Petersburg in 1908 and became very popular. The story of Nikolai Gogol/Mykola Hohol (1809-1852) is equally relevant here. Hohol published his first Russian-language book about village life in Ukraine, based on Ukrainian folklore, culture, and traditional motifs, titled "Evenings on the Farm near Dikanka" in St. Petersburg in 1831. It was a highly successful work.

The Valuev Circular of July 18th 1863 banned the use of the Little Russian (Ukrainian) language, including in publications and theatrical performances, in Ukraine, a ban that lasted until the Russian Revolution. After Russia's civil wars, in which the Bolsheviks frequently relied on the Red Army to gain control over Ukraine by force, a 1923 policy called *korenizatsiia* (indigenization) recognized the language and culture of each of the non-Russian republics created since 1917. After Lenin's death, Stalin implemented this measure because the Bolsheviks faced the challenge of ruling the Soviet Union and needed to recruit local cadres while preventing separatist nationalism from growing.

However, in the case of Ukraine, the Ukrainianization policy was effectively phased out starting in 1932 when a man-made famine (Holodomor) broke out. Ukrainian communist leader Mykola Skrypnyk (1872-1933), a pioneer of *korenizatsiia*, committed suicide in 1933. Stalin was already tightening the screws after 1928 because of the Five-Year Plan, and he had made clear even earlier that Ukraine could have cultural and educational autonomy but not serious economic or military power, as Ukrainian communist leader Oleksandr Shumsky (1890-1946) and others wanted. Most likely, Stalin was growing nervous about Ukraine's autonomous development getting out of hand even before the Holodomor, so he replaced some independently minded Bolsheviks like Ukrainian Shumsky with people loyal to the center, such as Lazar Kaganovich (1893-1991), who was Jewish. Also, korenizatsiia was not formally repealed, but its measures stopped being pursued and Stalin began to rehabilitate ethnic Russians as the leading nation of the Soviet Union.

During the 1920s, there was a major period of creative output for Ukrainian literature and art. Many Ukrainian writers like Mykola Khvylovy (1893-1933), Valerian Pidmohylny (1901-1937), Mykhail Semenko (1892-1937), Maik Yohansen (1895-1937), and Les Kurbas (1887-1937) published their ground-breaking books and made fantastic stage plays. Early Soviet Ukraine was a vibrant place in term of culture. Unfortunately, most of the ground-breaking Ukrainian writers, artists and intellectuals were killed during Stalin's purges in the 1930s.

Also, during the Soviet era, Ukrainian culture, folk songs, and dances were often regarded as Soviet culture for foreign propaganda and during 1970s and 1980s major Ukrainian choirs and dance groups went even to Japan advertising Soviet culture. That is why for a while Japanese audience thought that Ukrainian folksongs were Russian. However, displaying the blue and yellow flag was crossing the line. This was the flag of Symon Petliura, who was considered a traitor by the Soviet authorities. Still, many Ukrainian peasants and workers fought under the Soviet banner in 1917 to 1921 because it promised social liberation, even if many of them would later be persecuted under Stalin. The period of the 1920s was a fragile experiment in Ukrainian mass culture and art that got cut short when Stalin decided that it had grown into something threatening.

In other words, while local identities were exploited, nationalism was restricted. However, Petliura's nationalism was not the only option for Ukrainians living in the 1920s. Looking at national communists like Vasyl' Shakhrai (1888-1920) Serhiy

Mazlakh (1878-1937), Mykola Skrypnyk, and Oleksandr Shumsky, "Soviet power" (radians'ka vlada in Ukrainian) could be an attractive possibility despite the heavy-handed centralism of the Russian Bolsheviks, but it was ultimately Moscow that prevailed over more independent minds in Kharkiv and Kyiv after 1928. It is important to distinguish between the creativity and relative cultural autonomy of the mid-1920s and what came next in the form of purges and torture. Things once again changed under Nikita Khrushchev and, more fatefully, during Mikhail Gorbachev's reforms, which by 1990 opened the possibility of a looser Soviet Union including a sovereign Ukraine. Somewhat like the Hetmanate, Soviet Ukraine went through an extremely torturous but sometimes vibrant alternation between relative autonomy in creative endeavours and subjugation by the Russian center including moments in which some ethnic Ukrainians identified with the larger all-imperial ruling elite or the Soviet project.

Still, after many years of being unable to express one's identity freely, one inevitably learns the language, cultural code and behaviour of the winners and rulers and integrates into their society. Those losers who refused to join them would lose their lives, and there was no other way.

The Russia I have met

I remember back in the old days, I loved my Russian teacher in junior high school. She was a tall woman with a beautiful voice, Alla Petrovna. She had a great sense of humor, and even the naughty kids in the class enjoyed her jokes. Everyone laughed a lot during her classes. She was from the town of Yenakiieve, Donetsk region, in the eastern part of Ukraine, where the coal mining industry was flourishing. She was a strong woman who divorced her husband because he worked in the coal mines and drank a lot and was violent and abusive to the family. She moved to Kyiv with her two daughters. She is still active at almost 90 years old. She took refuge in Germany for a while during the war.

I enjoyed both the Russian literature we studied in her class and the essays she assigned to us. I wanted to read more, so my father, who worked for a publishing company, bought me many books that most people could not afford during the Soviet era. I curled up at home during the winter holidays to read romantic works of Alexander Pushkin, passionate novels of Mikhail Lermontov, Ivan Turgenev, whose writing was flowing like a river, Mikhail Prishvin, who depicted nature beautifully, Ivan Bunin, who skillfully wrote about love, and Konstantin Simonov, who wrote many poems about World War II. I was impressed by their books and will treasure them all my life. I never thought that all of them would be used for propaganda.

I have always loved Russian movies and have seen many of them. However, as the invasion progressed, a conversation in Nikita Mikhalkov's *The Barber of Siberia* came to mind. It goes like this:

- How is the value of life determined in Russia?
- It depends on whose life it is.

Indeed it is. Missiles have been launched at civilian homes, hospitals, and schools, killing many people. It seems to be a tradition of the old Russian Empire that has no respect for human life.

When I drank with my Russian friends in the days of peace, they would always ask me after the second drink, "Why did Ukraine and other republics become independent? It was good in Soviet Union, the country was much bigger and stronger." Every gathering was the same.

I also remember that when I published my first novel in Ukrainian, I was asked why. I was at a loss as to what to say. I can write in Russian as much as I like, but when it comes to some deep issues, such as love, friendship or home, it may be easier to express them in "the language you speak with your mother". You may laugh at this, however, I am sure you will understand what I want to say. I prefer to express my deepest thoughts with the words I learned from my mother.

I still have not discussed this topic with my Russian friends. Here's how it happened.

One of my students told me about the Bucha massacre. Her parents run a private nursing home, and since the atmosphere was dangerous even before the invasion began, they decided to send home the elderly who could walk. However, the bedridden elderly could not be moved. Since the building had a rather spacious basement, they brought food and other necessities there and lived in hiding for several weeks after the invasion. Fortunately, they were not found, and when they finally got out and visited their neighbors after the retreat of the Russian army, they hugged each other saying while crying: "We thought you were dead". They then learned of the massacre.

When I told this story to my Russian friend, his reply was not an apology but the following: "I don't doubt what you are saying. This is what war is like. The cultural exterior of man is peeled away to reveal his animal side. Unlike intellectuals like you and me, countrymen in both our countries tend to show their animal side. This is what happens when such a person picks up a machine gun. We will always be surrounded by these savages, so it is important to preserve our own humanity. Unfortunately there is nothing else we can do for now. Take care." To be honest, at that time in early April, I wanted him to apologize and comfort me, not to engage in some pompous philosophical discussion, but that did not happen. Since then, we have kept our relationship at the formal level of sending birthday messages to each other.

Affection for a country begins with affection for its people. Love is born from books and music written by locals. When civilians are killed in war by people of *that* country, feelings change.

The other day I had a chance to listen to a presentation by Volodymyr Paniotto, the most famous sociologist in Ukraine. Comparing the situation twenty years ago and after February 24th, 2022, the favorability of Russia and Russians has dropped from 90 to 34 percent.

Moreover, confidence in the Ukrainian government and military has increased. Compared to last August, the numbers have almost doubled: trust in the military has increased from 68 to 94 percent, in the president from 36 to 80 percent, and in the government from 18 to 35 percent. This is a big change for Ukrainians, who tend to distrust their government and officials.

One year has already passed since the invasion, and the residents of the apartment building on Lobanovskyy Boulevard, whose 19th and 20th floors were attacked, have repaired the damage by themselves and are still living there. Since the beginning of the war, I have not yet met with my Russian friends and we have not talked about this destruction.

Recently, I read over messages I received last winter. As it has been a while since I received them, I was calm as I read. Under normal circumstances, it would have been an usual conversation, however I wanted them to choose different words because of the war situation. I wish I could meet them once and talk about it. Their failure to speak up has created a society that allowed the Bucha massacre to happen. I am not sure if we will remain friends. Relationships between countries are based, in particular, on relationships between people. Even after this war is over, the trauma, the distrust and anger towards the other side will remain. We may not be able to talk as easily as we did in the past.

(February 28, 2023)

Conclusion
Thoughts of Ukrainians on Homeland and Borders

The Morning of February 24th

Less than three weeks after I published my book "Ukrainians Beyond Borders" (Gunzosha) on February 5th, 2022, Russia invaded Ukraine at 5:00 on the morning of February 24th. Missiles were launched at the apartment building next to my school, and the next day I had to evacuate my family from Kyiv.

Many Ukrainians, including my family, never imagined that they would be displaced beyond the border, as the title of my book suggests. Moreover, as a historian who was researching Ukrainian emigration and the Ukrainian diaspora, I never imagined that my research topic would become my life.

It has been more than a year since the Russian invasion began. According to the Ukrainian government, as of September 2022, 9 million Ukrainians had fled the country. As of now, more than 14 million Ukrainians are abroad. Hearing these staggering figures, you must realize that the war has not only caused the material damage you see on the news, but also the impacted the society and culture of Ukraine and, especially on its economy.

On February 24th, just before 5 a.m. when everyone was sleeping deeply, cities all over Ukraine were bombed. Many Ukrainians moved westward to save their lives. Later, when western Ukraine was also bombed and became unsafe, many began to seek sanctuary across the western border.

Since the time of the Cossacks, the western border has been more or less formed, at least in the minds of proponents of an ethnographic Ukraine like historian Mykhailo Hrushevsky, but the eastern one not so much. This time, just like during 1917-1921, Ukraine was attacked from the east and the north, yet the western border, which used to be tightly closed, magically opened probably for the first time this wide to save Ukrainian lives and let in those who wanted to cross the border. People without passports, just with some local Ukrainian IDs in cars or on foot, with dogs or cats, could cross the western border, saving the lives of many Ukrainians. Ukraine, which had been striving to join the EU, eventually entered the bloc at the level of individuals who began to live there as refugees.

This made me think again about homeland and borders, as well as about the history of my country and my family history.

Borders Determined by Others

The territory of Ukraine has enjoyed periods of Cossack freedom, like in the times of the Zaporizhzhian Sich and the Hetmanate, followed by periods of Polish, Russian, and Austro-Hungarian domination. The different ruling states practiced different degrees of repression. Ukrainians in Halychyna gained a favorable position under Habsburg rule and were able to develop a national movement much stronger and broadly based than the one in Russia. Also, Nazi Germany during World War II was responsible for some of the worst repression alongside the Soviet perpetrators of the Holodomor in Ukraine in the 1930s. For a long time, people from other countries have mapped and defined the borders of Ukraine.

This time, as in the days of its former empire, Russia is trying to redraw the borders of Ukraine. The road to the full-scale war of 2022 started with the annexation of Crimea in the spring of 2014, but at that time the international community underestimated the situation. They betrayed Ukraine since the Budapest Memorandum signed by powerful Western countries agreed to recognize Ukraine's borders. Russia then began the work on the separation of Donetsk and Luhansk regions from Ukraine. Admittedly, there were probably also many ethnic Russians who wanted to separate, echoing the demands of the Russian minority who demanded a separate Donetsk-Kryvyi Rih Republic in 1918 rather than joining Soviet Ukraine.

However, Ukraine has become an independent state twice in the last 100 years. The first such state was the Ukrainian People's

Republic, which was established in January 1918 and lasted two years, albeit with changes in government. After that, the country was occupied by the Soviet Union, and many politicians and intellectuals fled across the western border to Europe. Ordinary citizens had been fleeing the country until 1922, when the Soviet regime was almost consolidated. Many went from Odesa to Istanbul and upon arrival moved to Europe or the United States. Also, many Ukrainian peasants in Volhynia looked to Soviet Ukraine as a source of liberation from Poland, while numerous Ukrainian intellectuals stayed in the Soviet Union or returned later, like Hrushevsky. Thus, the traffic went in both directions.

The same was the case when, after the abolition of serfdom in 1861, the peasants were not satisfied with the plots of land they were given and went to settle in the Far East. Many Ukrainians migrated to the Far East and Siberia, where they amassed wealth. Those of them who did not want to live under the Soviet regime, established in 1922, also moved across the border to Harbin. Ukrainians have a long history of leaving the country not only for economic reasons, but also for political ones as well.

Unlike the Ukrainian People's Republic, the present Ukrainian state has experienced a lengthy period of independence. It became independent from the USSR on August 24th, 1991, and celebrated its 30th anniversary in the summer of 2021. Six months later Russia invaded. As in the beginning of the 20th century, many civilians tried to cross the border. Nevertheless, since people had experienced a free life in their own country, they no longer have the urge to live abroad.

Missiles flew from afar to their cities, and Ukrainians felt their lives were in immediate danger. Those who left the country early in the first days were lucky. Some of my friends stayed in shelters for a long time. These people almost became numb to danger.

Ukrainians, who have never desired to be brought back to the reality of the Soviet era, in the last thirty years have witnessed a generation that knows nothing of that time. People who had been studying in schools by the time the USSR had collapsed, have become politicians and even presidents. They are well aware of the difference between pre-independence freedom and the freedom after independence, no matter how much propaganda from the outside comes to them. Freedom of movement, to study a foreign language of your choice even if you are not a child of a Communist Party official, to go abroad and have a normal conversation with local people. Those who have discovered the freedom that they could not enjoy under the Soviet dictatorship can no longer return to the outdated authoritarian regime that impoverished the people and controlled them with the "correct" news on a TV with only one channel.

This war brought to Ukraine will be the last point of separation from the Soviet Union. Kharkiv and Sumy, who used to feel an affinity with Russia and are located near the Russian border, are now de-Russifying and rethinking their identity for the last time after experiencing heavy bombing. As we have seen, the Ukrainian view of Russia has rapidly deteriorated since the invasion began.

At the Border Between Austria and Hungary

At the beginning of this war, my Japanese friends told me: "Don't worry. You will definitely be able to live somewhere on Earth." That may be true, but in a way this experience is similar to the experience of the summer after the nuclear accident in Chornobyl in 1986.

At that time, I also left home with only the bare necessities in a small bag. I did not know if I would be able to go home again, but the significant difference this time was that I was no longer a child. I am no longer in the position of being taken care of. I take care of myself and make decisions. In the words of one of my acquaintances, our generation has suddenly been put in the front row of society, and we are still getting used to it.

As I mentioned in the section "A War of Men, Women and Children," the children's generation quickly made friends and learned foreign languages in the refugee centers. The children's drawings are often black-colored, and their war experiences are still dormant in their bodies. The elderly are different. They are suddenly moved from their settled lives to a different place and spend their days unaccustomed to their new life. When spring comes and it is time to sow the seeds in the fields, it is hard for some of the elderly who cannot go home, so they start to cry. Many of them utter curses when passing by gardening stores abroad. Ukrainians, for whom agriculture is an ingrained part of daily life, have been deprived not only of their homes, but also of important annual rituals.

When I took a train from Vienna to Budapest to meet my relatives in March 2022, I was impressed by the invisibility of European borders. Within an hour of leaving Vienna, the train approached the border and stopped in the middle of a field. A lively male voice announced: "Thank you for coming to Vienna. I hope you had an enjoyable time. We are now crossing the Hungarian border. Please come and visit us again." After a second of pause we departed without anyone coming to check our documents. I had never experienced such a pleasant border crossing. I cannot help but think that the EU is amazing. although the EU has made great strides toward embracing Ukraine these past few years, huge barriers still remain for others.

At Budapest station, volunteers were distributing blankets and food for Ukrainian refugees. Back in Vienna, railway workers were giving out tea and cookies, and staff of Caritas Internationalis (an international NGO) were offering places to live. Ukrainians were also moved by the fact that for a while the EU had made all trains in Europe free of charge for Ukrainian refugees.

The war has made me reconsider my feelings about the western and eastern borders of Ukraine. But unlike in the past, the eastern border, which was easy to pass through, suddenly has become a source of danger, while the western border has become a door to freedom.

A Place for This War in History

Recently, I have been asked what the historical significance of this war is for Ukraine. It is an interesting question and has several crucial layers. First of all, we need to consider the impact of the war on the self-consciousness of Ukrainians. It is also necessary to look not only at the first year of the war, but also at the past several hundred years.

The first Slavic state was the Principality of Kyiv, which existed from the 9th to the 13th century. There were other northern Russian principalities (Novgorod, Pskov) that were more democratic than Muscovy but ultimately got swallowed up. So, even within present-day Russia, there are regions that were independent and more trade-oriented around the same time as Kyiv emerged. The Grand Duchy of Moscow was established later, in the 13th century. Our people remained in Kyiv and did not flee anywhere. Now Russia is trying to take Kyiv. From Russia's point of view, without the history of the Principality of Kyiv, their history would start in the 13th century. They cannot allow their history to be shortened and their presence to be diminished. But from the Kyiv perspective, it is unforgivable that the "son" who once went out into the world, now is violently attacking the "parent."

In the 16th to 18th centuries, Ukrainian Cossacks fought and negotiated with neighboring Poland-Lithuania and the Ottoman Empire (also Sweden in Mazepa's time), trying to find a space for their people at the confluence of powerful empires. Bohdan Khmelnysky started out wanting to get the same rights for the Cossacks as the Polish szlachta had. He wasn't interested in social reforms and popular freedom in the beginning, at least until the lower classes unexpectedly joined his rebellion and convulsed Poland-Lithuania.

For Ukrainian Cossacks religion played a significant role in their choice of partners. However, their Orthodox coreligionists ultimately colonized the Cossacks, who had mistakenly thought that they would understand them the best and signed a treaty with the Russian Empire in 1654. While it is true that Ukraine became a Russian colony in the 18th and 19th centuries, many members of the upper strata of the Cossacks starshyna voluntarily married into Russian noble families. For that reason, populist historians of the 19th century criticized the Cossack elites for betraying the peasantry. Also, in Ukraine, there were generations of historians during Soviet time, and even after independence, who were uneasy to call that period "the colonial period." However, it is necessary to call it by its proper name and allow us to freely review the historical facts.

Poland-Lithuania enserfed Ukrainian peasants, and the Polish szlachta was brutal in extracting wealth from the lower classes. At the same time, serfdom was imposed by Muscovy on other Rus' principalities under Ivan Velikii and Ivan Groznyi, so there were plenty of ancestors of present-day Russians who were free farmers before then. Still, after Ukrainian territories were absorbed, the free-spirited Ukrainian farmers were also made serfs when their lands were taken away from them by the Russian Empire. This situation continued until 1861, and great socioeconomic pressure was exerted on them. However, most peasants in imperial Russia were not impacted by elite culture, so even Russification policies had limited effects on the ground, though they were far more intolerable for intellectuals in the cities. Despite the fact that Ukraine was not small at all in terms of territory, spirit, as well as hopes and dreams, it was named "Little Russia" (Malorossiya). Many Cossack elites and common people called themselves "Ruthenians" before the 19th century, when the Ukrainian historians reclaimed "Ukraina" to denote an ethnographic territory. Also, there was a sense that the "Malorossiya" taken from Poland-Lithuania was distinct from the more multiethnic Novorossiya in the south, though there were "Malorusy" living there.

The Ukrainian language spoken by the oppressed peasants also faced a demanding situation. The publication of printed materials in Ukrainian, especially educational and religious literature, was forbidden by the Valuev Circular of 1863. After that, printed materials in Ukrainian were published abroad, yet the Ems Ukaz of 1876 banned the import of such printed material into the Russian Empire, as well as translation, plays, musical scores, and performances in Ukrainian. This is why Habsburg Galicia became the main site of popular nation-building on the ground.

Education in Ukrainian was also prohibited. The Ukaz lasted until the Russian Revolution of 1917. This prohibition of local languages was not necessarily a universal feature of how empires have treated their colonies. For instance, the Habsburgs could be quite tolerant, and the British never outlawed the use of Hindi, while the Ottomans did not ban Arabic either.

Until the 19th century, maps of Ukrainian territory were made by people from other countries, and Ukrainians rarely talked about themselves. People and geographical names were of course Russianized. In other words, Ukraine was not allowed to be a storyteller.

Shift from Listener to Narrator

As we have shown, the first independent state was established in Ukraine in January 1918, a year following the Russian Revolution and also the Ukrainian Revolution in 1917.

However, within two following years, Ukraine was suppressed by the Bolsheviks and became a part of the Soviet Union. Having failed to stay independent, Ukraine became the losing side. Most of the politicians of the time like Volodymyr Vynnychenko fled the country and became involved in anti-Soviet activities, writing in their diaries what they had done wrong. One major conclusion was that although they were powerful as individuals, they lacked unity.

At the same time, Ukrainian Bolsheviks and communists like Oleksandr Shumsky, Vasyl' Shakhrai, and Serhiy Mazlakh were able to mobilize large groups of Ukrainian peasants that considered Petliura to be a pro-Polish traitor and wanted to immediately redistribute land, which the Directory did not do. This is not to excuse the Russian Bolsheviks but rather to point out that there were many Ukrainian revolutionaries who considered alignment with Moscow to be potentially preferable to membership in "Europe," partly because the Austrians and Germans had just invaded their homeland and replaced the Central Rada with Hetman Pavlo Skoropadsky.

Korenizatsiia during mid-1920s, for instance, was popular with Ukrainian revolutionaries and intellectuals within the Soviet Union. But later on, even though Ukrainian cultural activities were allowed in Soviet Union, political struggles for greater autonomy or independence were banned, and those who were still active in these currents were often repressed or even killed. The Ukrainian diaspora abroad created networks and fought; however, there was no way for them to win against the Soviet leviathan. The losing side cannot write the history books, so its story remains largely unknown. Despite the upheavals of emigration, Ukrainians secretly preserved their traditions, language, lifestyle, and culture, and passed them on from generation to generation.

When the Soviet Union collapsed in 1991, all Ukrainians were incredibly happy that they were able to gain independence peacefully. They did not think about the price their people had paid to achieve this moment when Ukraine was still part of the Russian Empire and the Soviet Union when they were struggling to make a living. From there, they have had 30 years of free life, and they have been taking care of their own way, despite problems they have faced. The economic problems continue under the oligarchs who kept power post-1991 in Ukraine. The death rates, murder rates, life expectancies, and per capita incomes were all discouraging in the first decade of independence, and even though conditions improved for some people, the country remained in dire straits economically. Unfortunately, European leaders did not exactly hurry to help to rebuild Ukraine like they did for Poland.

The recent invasion, especially the Bucha and Irpin massacres in February and March of 2022, and the crimes against civilians revealed after the liberation of the occupied areas, have awakened many years of dormant anger. Ukrainians, who came to live in fear of losing their lives and those of their families, are no longer listeners, but storytellers. One glance at the number of literary, artistic, musical works and journalistic articles that have emerged in protest of the Russian invasion is speaks for itself.

So far, Ukraine has not been a protagonist, playing a minor role in a story written by others. This time, I feel as if the characters who were not in a position to write history on the losing side suddenly became the lead roles and some sort of uneasiness in the heart, discomfort and restraint in talking about it are gone. Ukrainians now able to reevaluate their history and life and talk about it. They finally became the narrator of their own story.

As a result, progress is being made in recovering historical and artistic works that were previously considered to be Russian. Ukraine is in the spotlight and the international community cannot ignore it. As a result, Ilya Repin, a painter whose Cossack paintings are on display at the Museum of Fine Arts in New York, and Arkhip Kuindzhi, a landscape painter from Mariupol, have also been reaffirmed as Ukrainians. Most likely, Kuindzhi and Repin, like Mykola Hohol/Nikolai Gogol, inhabited multiple cultural worlds and saw their Ukrainian and Russian identities as connected. But their Ukrainian identity was always hiding in the background of the story. It never had a chance to step forward and be told. Now they are finally able to talk and to return home.

With this invasion, Ukraine is reassessing centuries of its past and is shifting from the losing side it has regained its identity and is telling its own story, which includes the history of the nation.

Home in our Hearts

The closest border to my summer house is the one with Belarus. It is only 150 kilometers away. In Tokyo terms, it is about the distance from Tokyo to Toshima in the Izu Islands. The British capital, meanwhile, is just 150 kilometers from Calais. What would the people of London do if they were attacked from Calais? Back in 1066, Britain was invaded by the Normans, and we know just how seriously it impacted the course of the island's history.

My family has lived in Kyiv for four generations. Before that, from the 18th century until the Russian Revolution, most of my family were farmers in the Chernihiv region bordering Belarus. Our house is still there, which I have been visiting every summer since I was a child, spending peaceful and happy times. In January 2022, just before the war started, when we were considering where to evacuate to in case of emergency, and we realized that this place would be invaded overnight. It would be a bad choice. Fortunately, the area was not occupied, but missile attacks continued, and the family next door seemed to have been living in their basement for a while. I spoke to them on the phone in the spring of 2022 and they said to me: "We don't know what will happen in the autumn, so We are thinking of planting potatoes just in case". I rented the land to them for free.

I could not go back there in the summer or autumn, but the family had some relatives evacuated from Kherson in the south, and the potatoes they had harvested at the end of August came in handy.

Having worked around the world, am used to living in a foreign country. Nevertheless, this experience is completely different. There is no way back home, so it is not a decision based on a free choice. When the decision is between home and survival, I will always choose the latter.

And yet, I did not think the war would last this long. As I wrote in the section "Ukraine and Japan," 2022 is the 30th anniversary of the establishment of diplomatic relations between Japan and Ukraine, and an online lecture by a former Japanese diplomat was scheduled for February 24th. I will never forget that when I called to notify him about the cancellation, he told me that "this war may go on for a long time." When I saw the videos of missiles being launched into the apartment building next to the school I attended as a child, I did not want to believe it, but I knew that this was the reality.

More than two and a half years has passed since then. I have colleagues and former students who have joined the armed forces, and friends and acquaintances who have taken refuge abroad. When I think of the number of outstanding researchers, athletes, businesspeople and professionals who lost their lives, I cannot stop my anger and tears. It saddens me to think of the suffering that children and the elderly are undergoing, of people who have been separated from their families and are trying their best to stay connected to their homeland through social networks.

Russia is a huge country and still wants the rich territory of a neighboring country of diligent people. Ukrainians are suffering because they have the courage to speak up about their distinct identity and that they are a different nation from Russians.

I am now reminded of a work by Fukuzawa Yukichi called "Datsu-A Ron" (sometimes translated as "Leaving Asia"). In the two decades after the Meiji Restoration, Fukuzawa was trying to reconfigure Japan's position the world by advocating that the Japanese at least mentally abandon an allegedly conservative Asia. The context may differ, yet over the past year Ukrainians have sharply turned toward thinking of parting ways with Russia, cutting themselves free from the big neighboring empire that they have relied on for so long. They have firmly identified their borders and decided not to give their homeland to anyone. It is obvious. For the Ukrainian people, this war is a crucial moment in which they will either disappear or survive. Recently, there have been voices in Japan saying that it is time to stop fighting and start peaceful negotiations. I don't think that Japanese people would do that if it their existence were questioned like that of the Ukrainians now.

This situation has made me think a lot about Japan's attitude towards peace and war. The Constitution of Japan emphasizes the renunciation of war as a means of settling international disputes. However, in the case of aggression, as in the case of Ukraine today, this principle is open to discussion. What would you do if you were living peacefully and then one day a bomb struck your home? What would you do if you and your family and friends would cease to exist if you did not protect yourself and them? Imagine how it is to live life under daily missile attacks from a neighboring country. If you cannot imagine this, download the Ukrainian "Air raid alarm" (*Povitryana Tryvoha* in Ukrainian) app and put it by your bed. In Japan, in the USA or in Europe, where peace is taken for granted, you will lose your ability sleep soundly in two days. Then you will understand the motivation of Ukrainians who are still fighting.

Recently in Japan, people have said: "I feel pity for Ukraine and Ukrainians." I have mixed feelings when I hear this. It is true that our country is experiencing tough times. However, thinking of ourselves as worthy of pity only makes us feel like victims, and nothing good will come of it. The Ukrainian people are fighting hard to protect their homeland, freedom and dignity, and they are trying to turn this trauma into a source of growth. Don't feel sorry for Ukrainians; instead, keep supporting them.

UKRAINIAN VOICES

Collected by Andreas Umland

1 *Mychailo Wynnyckyj*
   Ukraine's Maidan, Russia's War
   A Chronicle and Analysis of the Revolution of Dignity
   With a foreword by Serhii Plokhy
   ISBN 978-3-8382-1327-9

2 *Olexander Hryb*
   Understanding Contemporary Ukrainian and Russian Nationalism
   The Post-Soviet Cossack Revival and Ukraine's National Security
   With a foreword by Vitali Vitaliev
   ISBN 978-3-8382-1377-4

3 *Marko Bojcun*
   Towards a Political Economy of Ukraine
   Selected Essays 1990–2015
   With a foreword by John-Paul Himka
   ISBN 978-3-8382-1368-2

4 *Volodymyr Yermolenko (ed.)*
   Ukraine in Histories and Stories
   Essays by Ukrainian Intellectuals
   With a preface by Peter Pomerantsev
   ISBN 978-3-8382-1456-6

5 *Mykola Riabchuk*
   At the Fence of Metternich's Garden
   Essays on Europe, Ukraine, and Europeanization
   ISBN 978-3-8382-1484-9

6 *Marta Dyczok*
   Ukraine Calling
   A Kaleidoscope from Hromadske Radio 2016–2019
   With a foreword by Andriy Kulykov
   ISBN 978-3-8382-1472-6

7 *Olexander Scherba*
   Ukraine vs. Darkness
   Undiplomatic Thoughts
   With a foreword by Adrian Karatnycky
   ISBN 978-3-8382-1501-3

8 *Olesya Yaremchuk*
   Our Others
   Stories of Ukrainian Diversity
   With a foreword by Ostap Slyvynsky
   Translated from the Ukrainian by Zenia Tompkins and Hanna Leliv
   ISBN 978-3-8382-1475-7

9 *Nataliya Gumenyuk*
   Die verlorene Insel
   Geschichten von der besetzten Krim
   Mit einem Vorwort von Alice Bota
   Aus dem Ukrainischen übersetzt von Johann Zajaczkowski
   ISBN 978-3-8382-1499-3

10 *Olena Stiazhkina*
   Zero Point Ukraine
   Four Essays on World War II
   Translated from the Ukrainian by Svitlana Kulinska
   ISBN 978-3-8382-1550-1

11 *Oleksii Sinchenko, Dmytro Stus, Leonid Finberg (compilers)*
    Ukrainian Dissidents
    An Anthology of Texts
    ISBN 978-3-8382-1551-8

12 *John-Paul Himka*
    Ukrainian Nationalists and the Holocaust
    OUN and UPA's Participation in the Destruction of Ukrainian Jewry, 1941–1944
    ISBN 978-3-8382-1548-8

13 *Andrey Demartino*
    False Mirrors
    The Weaponization of Social Media in Russia's Operation to Annex Crimea
    With a foreword by Oleksiy Danilov
    ISBN 978-3-8382-1533-4

14 *Svitlana Biedarieva (ed.)*
    Contemporary Ukrainian and Baltic Art
    Political and Social Perspectives, 1991–2021
    ISBN 978-3-8382-1526-6

15 *Olesya Khromeychuk*
    A Loss
    The Story of a Dead Soldier Told by His Sister
    With a foreword by Andrey Kurkov
    ISBN 978-3-8382-1570-9

16 *Marieluise Beck (Hg.)*
    Ukraine verstehen
    Auf den Spuren von Terror und Gewalt
    Mit einem Vorwort von Dmytro Kuleba
    ISBN 978-3-8382-1653-9

17 *Stanislav Aseyev*
    Heller Weg
    Geschichte eines Konzentrationslagers im Donbass 2017–2019
    Aus dem Russischen übersetzt von Martina Steis und Charis Haska
    ISBN 978-3-8382-1620-1

18 *Mykola Davydiuk*
    Wie funktioniert Putins Propaganda?
    Anmerkungen zum Informationskrieg des Kremls
    Aus dem Ukrainischen übersetzt von Christian Weise
    ISBN 978-3-8382-1628-7

19 *Olesya Yaremchuk*
    Unsere Anderen
    Geschichten ukrainischer Vielfalt
    Aus dem Ukrainischen übersetzt von Christian Weise
    ISBN 978-3-8382-1635-5

20 *Oleksandr Mykhed*
    „Dein Blut wird die Kohle tränken"
    Über die Ostukraine
    Aus dem Ukrainischen übersetzt von Simon Muschick und Dario Planert
    ISBN 978-3-8382-1648-5

21 *Vakhtang Kipiani (Hg.)*
    Der Zweite Weltkrieg in der Ukraine
    Geschichte und Lebensgeschichten
    Aus dem Ukrainischen übersetzt von Margarita Grinko
    ISBN 978-3-8382-1622-5

22 *Vakhtang Kipiani (ed.)*
    World War II, Uncontrived and Unredacted
    Testimonies from Ukraine
    Translated from the Ukrainian by Zenia Tompkins and Daisy Gibbons
    ISBN 978-3-8382-1621-8

23 Dmytro Stus
Vasyl Stus
Life in Creativity
Translated from the Ukrainian by
Ludmila Bachurina
ISBN 978-3-8382-1631-7

24 Vitalii Ogiienko (Ed.)
The Holodomor and the
Origins of the Soviet Man
Reading the Testimony of
Anastasia Lysyvets
With forewords by Natalka
Bilotserkivets and Serhy
Yekelchyk
Translated from the Ukrainian by
Alla Parkhomenko and
Alexander J. Motyl
ISBN 978-3-8382-1616-4

25 Vladislav Davidzon
Jewish-Ukrainian Relations
and the Birth of a Political
Nation
Selected Writings 2013-2021
With a foreword by Bernard-
Henri Lévy
ISBN 978-3-8382-1509-9

26 Serhy Yekelchyk
Writing the Nation
The Ukrainian Historical
Profession in Independent
Ukraine and the Diaspora
ISBN 978-3-8382-1695-9

27 Ildi Eperjesi, Oleksandr
Kachura
Shreds of War
Fates from the Donbas Frontline
2014-2019
With a foreword by Olexiy
Haran
ISBN 978-3-8382-1680-5

28 Oleksandr Melnyk
World War II as an Identity
Project
Historicism, Legitimacy
Contests, and the (Re-)Con-
struction of Political Commu-
nities in Ukraine, 1939–1946
With a foreword by David R.
Marples
ISBN 978-3-8382-1704-8

29 Olesya Khromeychuk
Ein Verlust
Die Geschichte eines gefallenen
ukrainischen Soldaten, erzählt
von seiner Schwester
Mit einem Vorwort von Andrej
Kurkow
Aus dem Englischen übersetzt
von Lily Sophie
ISBN 978-3-8382-1770-3

30 Tamara Martsenyuk,
Tetiana Kostiuchenko (eds.)
Russia's War in Ukraine
During 2022
Personal Experiences of
Ukrainian Scholars
ISBN 978-3-8382-1757-4

31 Ildikó Eperjesi, Oleksandr
Kachura
Shreds of War. Vol. 2
Fates from Crimea 2015–2022
With an interview of Oleh
Sentsov
ISBN 978-3-8382-1780-2

32 Yuriy Lukanov
The Press
How Russia Destroyed Media
Freedom in Crimea
With a foreword by Taras Kuzio
ISBN 978-3-8382-1784-0

33 Megan Buskey
Ukraine Is Not Dead Yet
A Family Story of Exile and
Return
ISBN 978-3-8382-1691-1

34 *Vira Ageyeva*
Behind the Scenes of the Empire
Essays on Cultural Relationships between Ukraine and Russia
With a foreword by Oksana Zabuzhko
ISBN 978-3-8382-1748-2

35 *Marieluise Beck (Ed.)*
Understanding Ukraine
Tracing the Roots of Terror and Violence
With a foreword by Dmytro Kuleba
ISBN 978-3-8382-1773-4

36 *Olesya Khromeychuk*
A Loss
The Story of a Dead Soldier Told by His Sister, 2nd edn.
With a foreword by Philippe Sands
With a preface by Andrii Kurkov
ISBN 978-3-8382-1870-0

37 *Taras Kuzio, Stefan Jajecznyk-Kelman*
Fascism and Genocide
Russia's War Against Ukrainians
ISBN 978-3-8382-1791-8

38 *Alina Nychyk*
Ukraine Vis-à-Vis Russia and the EU
Misperceptions of Foreign Challenges in Times of War, 2014–2015
With a foreword by Paul D'Anieri
ISBN 978-3-8382-1767-3

39 *Sasha Dovzhyk (ed.)*
Ukraine Lab
Global Security, Environment, and Disinformation Through the Prism of Ukraine
With a foreword by Rory Finnin
ISBN 978-3-8382-1805-2

40 *Serhiy Kvit*
Media, History, and Education
Three Ways to Ukrainian Independence
With a preface by Diane Francis
ISBN 978-3-8382-1807-6

41 *Anna Romandash*
Women of Ukraine
Reportages from the War and Beyond
ISBN 978-3-8382-1819-9

42 *Dominika Rank*
Matzewe in meinem Garten
Abenteuer eines jüdischen Heritage-Touristen in der Ukraine
ISBN 978-3-8382-1810-6

43 *Myroslaw Marynowytsch*
Das Universum hinter dem Stacheldraht
Memoiren eines sowjet-ukrainischen Dissidenten
Mit einem Vorwort von Timothy Snyder und einem Nachwort von Max Hartmann
ISBN 978-3-8382-1806-9

44 *Konstantin Sigow*
Für Deine und meine Freiheit
Europäische Revolutions- und Kriegserfahrungen im heutigen Kyjiw
Mit einem Vorwort von Karl Schlögel
Herausgegeben von Regula M. Zwahlen
ISBN 978-3-8382-1755-0

45 *Kateryna Pylypchuk*
The War that Changed Us
Ukrainian Novellas, Poems, and Essays from 2022
With a foreword by Victor Yushchenko
Paperback
ISBN 978-3-8382-1859-5
Hardcover
ISBN 978-3-8382-1860-1

46 Kyrylo Tkachenko
    Rechte Tür Links
    Radikale Linke in Deutschland,
    die Revolution und der Krieg in
    der Ukraine, 2013-2018
    ISBN 978-3-8382-1711-6

47 Alexander Strashny
    The Ukrainian Mentality
    An Ethno-Psychological,
    Historical and Comparative
    Exploration
    With a foreword by Antonina
    Lovochkina
    Translated from the Ukrainian
    by Michael M. Naydan and
    Olha Tytarenko
    ISBN 978-3-8382-1886-1

48 Alona Shestopalova
    From Screens to Battlefields
    Tracing the Construction of
    Enemies on Russian Television
    With a foreword by Nina
    Jankowicz
    ISBN 978-3-8382-1884-7

49 Iaroslav Petik
    Politics and Society in the
    Ukrainian People's Republic
    (1917–1921) and
    Contemporary Ukraine
    (2013–2022)
    A Comparative Analysis
    With a foreword by Mykola
    Doroshko
    ISBN 978-3-8382-1817-5

50 Serhii Plokhy
    Der Mann mit der
    Giftpistole
    Eine Spionagegeschichte aus dem
    Kalten Krieg
    ISBN 978-3-8382-1789-5

51 Vakhtang Kipiani
    Ukrainische Dissidenten
    unter der Sowjetmacht
    Im Kampf um Wahrheit und
    Freiheit
    Aus dem Ukrainischen übersetzt
    von Christian Weise
    ISBN 978-3-8382-1890-8

52 Dmytro Shestakov
    When Businesses Test
    Hypotheses
    A Four-Step Approach to Risk
    Management for Innovative
    Startups
    With a foreword by Anthony J.
    Tether
    ISBN 978-3-8382-1883-0

53 Larissa Babij
    A Kind of Refugee
    The Story of an American Who
    Refused to Leave Ukraine
    With a foreword by Vladislav
    Davidzon
    ISBN 978-3-8382-1898-4

54 Julia Davis
    In Their Own Words
    How Russian Propagandists
    Reveal Putin's Intentions
    With a foreword by Timothy
    Snyder
    ISBN 978-3-8382-1909-7

55 Sonya Atlantova, Oleksandr
    Klymenko
    Icons on Ammo Boxes
    Painting Life on the Remnants of
    Russia's War in Donbas, 2014-21
    Translated from the Ukrainian by
    Anastasya Knyazhytska
    ISBN 978-3-8382-1892-2

56 Leonid Ushkalov
    Catching an Elusive Bird
    The Life of Hryhorii Skovoroda
    Translated from the Ukrainian
    by Natalia Komarova
    ISBN 978-3-8382-1894-6

57 Vakhtang Kipiani
    Ein Land weiblichen
    Geschlechts
    Ukrainische Frauenschicksale
    im 20. und 21. Jahrhundert
    Aus dem Ukrainischen übersetzt
    von Christian Weise
    ISBN 978-3-8382-1891-5

58 Petro Rychlo
„Zerrissne Saiten einer
überlauten Harfe ..."
Deutschjüdische Dichter der
Bukowina
ISBN 978-3-8382-1893-9

59 Volodymyr Paniotto
Sociology in Jokes
An Entertaining Introduction
ISBN 978-3-8382-1857-1

60 Josef Wallmannsberger (ed.)
Executing Renaissances
The Poetological Nation of Ukraine
ISBN 978-3-8382-1741-3

61 Pavlo Kazarin
The Wild West of Eastern Europe
A Ukrainian Guide on Breaking Free from Empire
Translated from the Ukrainian by Dominique Hoffman
ISBN 978-3-8382-1842-7

62 Ernest Gyidel
Ukrainian Public Nationalism in the General Government
The Case of Krakivski Visti, 1940–1944
With a foreword by David R. Marples
ISBN 978-3-8382-1865-6

63 Olexander Hryb
Understanding Contemporary Russian Militarism
From Revolutionary to New Generation Warfare
With a foreword by Mark Laity
ISBN 978-3-8382-1927-1

64 Orysia Hrudka, Bohdan Ben
Dark Days, Determined People
Stories from Ukraine under Siege
With a foreword by Myroslav Marynovych
ISBN 978-3-8382-1958-5

65 Oleksandr Pankieiev (ed.)
Narratives of the Russo-Ukrainian War
A Look Within and Without
With a foreword by Natalia Khanenko-Friesen
ISBN 978-3-8382-1964-6

66 Roman Sohn, Ariana Gic (eds.)
Unrecognized War
The Fight for Truth about Russia's War on Ukraine
With a foreword by Viktor Yushchenko
ISBN 978-3-8382-1947-9

67 Paul Robert Magocsi
Ukraina Redux
Schon wieder die Ukraine ...
ISBN 978-3-8382-1942-4

68 Paul Robert Magocsi
L'Ucraina Ritrovata
Sullo Stato e l'Identità Nazionale
ISBN 978-3-8382-1982-0

69 Max Hartmann
Ein Schrei der Verzweiflung
Aquarelle von Danylo Movchan zu Russlands Krieg in der Ukraine
Mit einem Vorwort von Mateusz Sora
Paperback
ISBN 978-3-8382-2011-6
Hardcover
ISBN 978-3-8382-2012-3

70 Vakhtang Kebuladze (Hg.)
Die Zukunft, die wir uns wünschen
Essays aus der Ukraine
ISBN 978-3-8382-1531-0

71 Marieluise Beck, Jan Claas Behrends, Gelinada Grinchenko und Oksana Mikheieva (Hgg.)
Deutsch-ukrainische Geschichten
Bruchstücke aus einer gemeinsamen Vergangenheit
ISBN 978-3-8382-2053-6

72 Pavlo Kazarin
Der Wilde Westen Ost-Europas
Der ukrainische Weg aus dem Imperium
Aus dem Ukrainischen übersetzt von Christian Weise
ISBN 978-3-8382-1843-4

73 Radomyr Mokryk
Die ukrainischen »Sechziger«
Chronologie einer Revolte
ISBN 978-3-8382-1873-1

74 Leonid Finberg
My Ukraine
Rethinking the Past, Building the Present
ISBN 978-3-8382-1974-5

75 Joseph Zissels
Consider My Inmost Thoughts
Essays, Lectures, and Interviews on Ukrainian Matters at the Turn of the Century
ISBN 978-3-8382-1975-2

76 Margarita Yehorchenko, Iryna Berlyand, Ihor Vinokurov (eds.)
Jewish Addresses in Ukraine
A Guide-Book
With a foreword by Leonid Finberg
ISB 978-3-8382-1976-9

77 Viktoriia Grivina
Kharkiv—A War City
A Collection of Essays from 2022–23
ISBN 978-3-8382-1988-2

78 Hjørdis Clemmensen, Viktoriia Grivina, Vasylysa Shchogoleva
Kharkiv Is a Dream
Public Art and Activism 2013–2023
With a foreword by Bohdan Volynskyi
ISBN 978-3-8382-2005-5

79 Olga Khomenko
The Faraway Sky of Kyiv
Ukrainians in the War
With a foreword by Hiroaki Kuromiya
ISBN 978-3-8382-2006-2

80 Daria Mattingly, Jonathon Vsetecka (eds.)
The Holodomor in Global Perspective
How the Famine in Ukraine Shaped the World
With a foreword by Anne Applebaum
ISBN 978-3-8382-1953-0

81 Olga Khomenko
Ukrainians beyond Borders
Nine Life Journeys Through the History of Eastern Europe
With a foreword by Zbigniew Wojnowski
ISBN 978-3-8382-2007-9

82 Mykhailo Minakov
From Servant to Leader
Chronicles of Ukraine under the Zelensky Presidency, 2019–2024
With a foreword by John Lloyd
ISBN 978-3-8382-2002-4

83 Volodymyr Hromov (ed.)
A Ruined Home
Sketches of War, 2022–2023
ISBN 978-3-8382-2008-6

84 Olha Tatokhina (ed.)
   Why Do They Kill Our People?
   Russia's War Against Ukraine as
   Told by Ukrainians
   With a foreword by Volodymyr
   Yermolenko
   ISBN 978-3-8382-2056-7

Book series "Ukrainian Voices"

Coordinator
Andreas Umland, National University of Kyiv-Mohyla Academy

Editorial Board
Lesia Bidochko, National University of Kyiv-Mohyla Academy
Svitlana Biedarieva, George Washington University, DC, USA
Ivan Gomza, Kyiv School of Economics, Ukraine
Natalie Jaresko, Aspen Institute, Kyiv/Washington
Olena Lennon, University of New Haven, West Haven, USA
Kateryna Yushchenko, First Lady of Ukraine 2005-2010, Kyiv
Oleksandr Zabirko, University of Regensburg, Germany

Advisory Board

Iuliia Bentia, National Academy of Arts of Ukraine, Kyiv
Natalya Belitser, Pylyp Orlyk Institute for Democracy, Kyiv
Oleksandra Bienert, Humboldt University of Berlin, Germany
Sergiy Bilenky, Canadian Institute of Ukrainian Studies, Toronto
Tymofii Brik, Kyiv School of Economics, Ukraine
Olga Brusylovska, Mechnikov National University, Odesa
Mariana Budjeryn, Harvard University, Cambridge, USA
Volodymyr Bugrov, Shevchenko National University, Kyiv
Olga Burlyuk, University of Amsterdam, The Netherlands
Yevhen Bystrytsky, NAS Institute of Philosophy, Kyiv
Andrii Danylenko, Pace University, New York, USA
Vladislav Davidzon, Atlantic Council, Washington/Paris
Mykola Davydiuk, Think Tank "Polityka," Kyiv
Andrii Demartino, National Security and Defense Council, Kyiv
Vadym Denisenko, Ukrainian Institute for the Future, Kyiv
Oleksandr Donii, Center for Political Values Studies, Kyiv
Volodymyr Dubovyk, Mechnikov National University, Odesa
Volodymyr Dubrovskiy, CASE Ukraine, Kyiv
Diana Dutsyk, National University of Kyiv-Mohyla Academy
Marta Dyczok, Western University, Ontario, Canada
Yevhen Fedchenko, National University of Kyiv-Mohyla Academy
Sofiya Filonenko, State Pedagogical University of Berdyansk
Oleksandr Fisun, Karazin National University, Kharkiv
Oksana Forostyna, Webjournal "Ukraina Moderna," Kyiv
Roman Goncharenko, Broadcaster "Deutsche Welle," Bonn
George Grabowicz, Harvard University, Cambridge, USA
Gelinada Grinchenko, Karazin National University, Kharkiv
Kateryna Härtel, Federal Union of European Nationalities, Brussels
Nataliia Hendel, University of Geneva, Switzerland
Anton Herashchenko, Kyiv School of Public Administration
John-Paul Himka, University of Alberta, Edmonton
Ola Hnatiuk, National University of Kyiv-Mohyla Academy
Oleksandr Holubov, Broadcaster "Deutsche Welle," Bonn
Yaroslav Hrytsak, Ukrainian Catholic University, Lviv
Oleksandra Humenna, National University of Kyiv-Mohyla Academy
Tamara Hundorova, NAS Institute of Literature, Kyiv
Oksana Huss, University of Bologna, Italy
Oleksandra Iwaniuk, University of Warsaw, Poland
Mykola Kapitonenko, Shevchenko National University, Kyiv
Georgiy Kasianov, Marie Curie-Skłodowska University, Lublin
Vakhtang Kebuladze, Shevchenko National University, Kyiv
Natalia Khanenko-Friesen, University of Alberta, Edmonton
Victoria Khiterer, Millersville University of Pennsylvania, USA
Oksana Kis, NAS Institute of Ethnology, Lviv
Pavlo Klimkin, Center for National Resilience and Development, Kyiv
Oleksandra Kolomiiets, Center for Economic Strategy, Kyiv

Sergiy Korsunsky, Kobe Gakuin University, Japan
Nadiia Koval, Kyiv School of Economics, Ukraine
Volodymyr Kravchenko, University of Alberta, Edmonton
Oleksiy Kresin, NAS Koretskiy Institute of State and Law, Kyiv
Anatoliy Kruglashov, Fedkovych National University, Chernivtsi
Andrey Kurkov, PEN Ukraine, Kyiv
Ostap Kushnir, Lazarski University, Warsaw
Taras Kuzio, National University of Kyiv-Mohyla Academy
Serhii Kvit, National University of Kyiv-Mohyla Academy
Yuliya Ladygina, The Pennsylvania State University, USA
Yevhen Mahda, Institute of World Policy, Kyiv
Victoria Malko, California State University, Fresno, USA
Yulia Marushevska, Security and Defense Center (SAND), Kyiv
Myroslav Marynovych, Ukrainian Catholic University, Lviv
Oleksandra Matviichuk, Center for Civil Liberties, Kyiv
Mykhailo Minakov, Kennan Institute, Washington, USA
Anton Moiseienko, The Australian National University, Canberra
Alexander Motyl, Rutgers University-Newark, USA
Vlad Mykhnenko, University of Oxford, United Kingdom
Vitalii Ogiienko, Ukrainian Institute of National Remembrance, Kyiv
Olga Onuch, University of Manchester, United Kingdom
Olesya Ostrovska, Museum "Mystetskyi Arsenal," Kyiv
Anna Osypchuk, National University of Kyiv-Mohyla Academy
Oleksandr Pankieiev, University of Alberta, Edmonton
Oleksiy Panych, Publishing House "Dukh i Litera," Kyiv
Valerii Pekar, Kyiv-Mohyla Business School, Ukraine
Yohanan Petrovsky-Shtern, Northwestern University, Chicago
Serhii Plokhy, Harvard University, Cambridge, USA
Andrii Portnov, Viadrina University, Frankfurt-Oder, Germany
Maryna Rabinovych, Kyiv School of Economics, Ukraine
Valentyna Romanova, Institute of Developing Economies, Tokyo
Natalya Ryabinska, Collegium Civitas, Warsaw, Poland

Darya Tsymbalyk, University of Oxford, United Kingdom
Vsevolod Samokhvalov, University of Liege, Belgium
Orest Semotiuk, Franko National University, Lviv
Viktoriya Sereda, NAS Institute of Ethnology, Lviv
Anton Shekhovtsov, University of Vienna, Austria
Andriy Shevchenko, Media Center Ukraine, Kyiv
Oxana Shevel, Tufts University, Medford, USA
Pavlo Shopin, National Pedagogical Dragomanov University, Kyiv
Karina Shyrokykh, Stockholm University, Sweden
Nadja Simon, freelance interpreter, Cologne, Germany
Olena Snigova, NAS Institute for Economics and Forecasting, Kyiv
Ilona Solohub, Analytical Platform "VoxUkraine," Kyiv
Iryna Solonenko, LibMod - Center for Liberal Modernity, Berlin
Galyna Solovei, National University of Kyiv-Mohyla Academy
Sergiy Stelmakh, NAS Institute of World History, Kyiv
Olena Stiazhkina, NAS Institute of the History of Ukraine, Kyiv
Dmitri Stratievski, Osteuropa Zentrum (OEZB), Berlin
Dmytro Stus, National Taras Shevchenko Museum, Kyiv
Frank Sysyn, University of Toronto, Canada
Olha Tokariuk, Center for European Policy Analysis, Washington
Olena Tregub, Independent Anti-Corruption Commission, Kyiv
Hlib Vyshlinsky, Centre for Economic Strategy, Kyiv
Mychailo Wynnyckyj, National University of Kyiv-Mohyla Academy
Yelyzaveta Yasko, NGO "Yellow Blue Strategy," Kyiv
Serhy Yekelchyk, University of Victoria, Canada
Victor Yushchenko, President of Ukraine 2005-2010, Kyiv
Oleksandr Zaitsev, Ukrainian Catholic University, Lviv
Kateryna Zarembo, National University of Kyiv-Mohyla Academy
Yaroslav Zhalilo, National Institute for Strategic Studies, Kyiv
Sergei Zhuk, Ball State University at Muncie, USA
Alina Zubkovych, Nordic Ukraine Forum, Stockholm
Liudmyla Zubrytska, National University of Kyiv-Mohyla Academy

Friends of the Series

Ana Maria Abulescu, University of Bucharest, Romania
Łukasz Adamski, Centrum Mieroszewskiego, Warsaw
Marieluise Beck, LibMod—Center for Liberal Modernity, Berlin
Marc Berensen, King's College London, United Kingdom
Johannes Bohnen, BOHNEN Public Affairs, Berlin
Karsten Brüggemann, University of Tallinn, Estonia
Ulf Brunnbauer, Leibniz Institute (IOS), Regensburg
Martin Dietze, German-Ukrainian Culture Society, Hamburg
Gergana Dimova, Florida State University, Tallahassee/London
Caroline von Gall, Goethe University, Frankfurt-Main
Zaur Gasimov, Rhenish Friedrich Wilhelm University, Bonn
Armand Gosu, University of Bucharest, Romania
Thomas Grant, University of Cambridge, United Kingdom
Gustav Gressel, European Council on Foreign Relations, Berlin
Rebecca Harms, European Centre for Press & Media Freedom, Leipzig
André Härtel, Stiftung Wissenschaft und Politik, Berlin/Brussels
Marcel Van Herpen, The Cicero Foundation, Maastricht
Richard Herzinger, freelance analyst, Berlin
Mieste Hotopp-Riecke, ICATAT, Magdeburg
Nico Lange, Munich Security Conference, Berlin
Martin Malek, freelance analyst, Vienna
Ingo Mannteufel, Broadcaster "Deutsche Welle," Bonn
Carlo Masala, Bundeswehr University, Munich
Wolfgang Mueller, University of Vienna, Austria
Dietmar Neutatz, Albert Ludwigs University, Freiburg
Torsten Oppelland, Friedrich Schiller University, Jena
Niccolò Pianciola, University of Padua, Italy
Gerald Praschl, German-Ukrainian Forum (DUF), Berlin
Felix Riefer, Think Tank Ideenagentur-Ost, Düsseldorf
Stefan Rohdewald, University of Leipzig, Germany
Sebastian Schäffer, Institute for the Danube Region (IDM), Vienna
Felix Schimansky-Geier, Friedrich Schiller University, Jena
Ulrich Schneckener, University of Osnabrück, Germany
Winfried Schneider-Deters, freelance analyst, Heidelberg/Kyiv
Gerhard Simon, University of Cologne, Germany
Kai Struve, Martin Luther University, Halle/Wittenberg
David Stulik, European Values Center for Security Policy, Prague
Andrzej Szeptycki, University of Warsaw, Poland
Philipp Ther, University of Vienna, Austria
Stefan Troebst, University of Leipzig, Germany

[Please send requests for changes in, corrections of, and additions to, this list to andreas.umland@stanforalumni.org.]

***ibidem*.eu**